DISCOVER THE RIGHT JOB FOR YOU!

Other books by Drs. Ron and Caryl Krannich

The Almanac of American Government Jobs and Careers
The Almanac of International Jobs and Careers
Careering and Re-Careering for the 1990s
The Complete Guide to International Jobs and Careers
The Complete Guide to Public Employment
Dynamite Cover Letters
Dynamite Resumes
The Educator's Guide to Alternative Jobs and Careers
Find a Federal Job Fast!
High Impact Resumes and Letters (with William Banis)
Interview for Success
Mayors and Managers
Moving Out of Education (with William Banis)
Moving Out of Government
Network Your Way to Job and Career Success
The Politics of Family Planning Policy
Re-Careering in Turbulent Times
Salary Success
Shopping in Exciting Australia and Papua New Guinea
Shopping in Exotic Places (with Jo Reimer)
Shopping the Exotic South Pacific
Shopping and Traveling in Exotic Asia
Shopping and Traveling in Exotic Hong Kong (with Jo Reimer)
Shopping and Traveling in Exotic Indonesia
Shopping and Traveling in Exotic Singapore and Malaysia
Shopping and Traveling in Exotic Thailand
Shopping and Traveling in the Exotic Philippines

DISCOVER THE RIGHT JOB FOR YOU!

Ronald L. Krannich, Ph.D.
Caryl Rae Krannich, Ph.D.

IMPACT PUBLICATIONS
Woodbridge, VA

DISCOVER THE RIGHT JOB FOR YOU! A Guide to Creating Job and Career Success

Copyright © 1991 by Ronald L. Krannich and Caryl Rae Krannich

All rights reserved. Printed in the United States of America. No part of this book may be used or reproduced in any manner whatsoever without written permission of the publisher: IMPACT PUBLICATIONS, 4580 Sunshine Court, Woodbridge, VA 22192, Tel. 703/361-7300.

Library of Congress Cataloguing-in-Publication Data

Krannich, Ronald L.
    Discover the right job for you! / Ronald L. Krannich, Caryl Rae Krannich
         p. cm.
    Includes bibliographical references and index.
    ISBN 0-942710-32-0. -- ISBN 0-942710-33-9 (pbk.)
    1. Job hunting. 2. Vocational interests. I. Krannich, Caryl Rae. II. Title
HF5382.K69 1991
650.14--dc20   90-21451
                                                               CIP

For information on distribution or quantity discount rates, Tel. 703/361-7300, FAX 703/335-9486, or write to: Sales Department, IMPACT PUBLICATIONS, 4580 Sunshine Court, Woodbridge, VA 22192. Distributed to the trade by National Book Network, 4720 Boston Way, Suite A, Lanham, MD 20706, Tel. 301/459-8696.

CONTENTS

Preface vii

CHAPTER ONE
Do First Things First 1
    Finding the Right Job 1
    A Job Fit For You 3
    Get Organized For Success 4
    Where Do You Go From Here? 7

CHAPTER TWO
Identify Your Careering Competencies 9
    Careering Competencies 9
    Adding It Up 12

CHAPTER THREE
Understand the Job Finding Process 13
    Finding Jobs 13
    The Career Development Process 15
    Organize and Sequence Your Job Search 19

CHAPTER FOUR
Seek Professional Assistance When Necessary 21
    Options 21
    Potential Pitfalls 22
    Alternative Services 23
    Choose the Best 28

CHAPTER FIVE
Alternative Choices and the Right "Fit" 30
    Alternative Approaches 30
    Beware of Underlying Assumptions 32
    A Job Targeted Approach 34
    Ask the Right Questions 35

CHAPTER SIX
What You Do Well: Skills and Abilities 38
    Know Your Skills 38
    Types of Skills 39
    Your Strengths 41
    Ask the Right Questions 41
    Functional/Transferable Skills 43
    Checklist Method 46
    Skills Map 46
    Autobiography of Accomplishments 47
    Computerized Skills Assessment Systems 48

CHAPTER SEVEN
What You Enjoy Doing: Interests and Values 49
    Work Interests 49
    Work Values 55
    Computerized Systems 62
    Your Future as Objectives 63

CHAPTER EIGHT
Identify Your Motivated Abilities and Skills (MAS) 64
    What's Your MAS? 64
    The Skills Map 65
    Autobiography of Accomplishments 66
    Motivated Skills Exercise 67
    Other Alternatives 74
    Benefit From Redundancy 74

CHAPTER NINE
Beyond Self-Knowledge to Self-Transformation 76
    From Self-Assessment to Self-Transformation 77
    Change 78
    Breakthrough Thinking 78
    The Art of Being Unrealistic 79
    Learning New Abilities and Skills 82
    Never Settle For Your Past 83
    Acquiring More Education and Training 83
    Become an Informed Consumer 91

CHAPTER TEN
Set Goals and State Your Objective 96
    Examine Your Past, Present, and Future 97
    Orient Yourself Toward the Needs of Employers 97
    Be Purposeful and Realistic 98
    Project Yourself Into the Future 99
    State a Functional Objective 117

CHAPTER ELEVEN
Alternative Jobs and Careers 122
    Linkage Systems 122
    Computer Programs 131
    Conduct Research 132
    Contact Organizations and People for Information 136
    Network for Information, Advice, and Referrals 137

CHAPTER TWELVE
Use Time and Plan Effectively 138
    When in Doubt, Take Action 138
    Use Time Wisely 139
    Plan to Take Action 144

CHAPTER THIRTEEN
Develop Strategies For Success 147

CHAPTER FOURTEEN
Discover the Right Resources 151
- Choosing What's Best For You 152
- What You Get 153
- Bibliography 159

Index 173

Career Resources 177

PREFACE

Millions of people each year find jobs and change careers. Some are more successful than others in finding the right job for them. For some, the process is relatively easy and results in rewarding jobs. For others, the process is painful and yields less than satisfactory results.

If you are looking for a job or contemplating a career change, this is a good time to take stock of your interests, values, abilities, skills, and goals **before** writing resumes, responding to job listings, or networking for job information. Unfortunately, many job seekers do last things first and thereby neglect to address the **basics** of the job finding process. This should not happen to you.

This book is all about doing first things first -- assessing your interests, values, abilities, skills, stating your goals, and relating this information about yourself to specific jobs before going on to other job search steps that ultimately result in job interviews and offers. For the key to job search success lies in yourself -- knowing who you are and what you want to do in reference to the world of work. You must answer important questions about yourself before you can communicate your qualifications and aspirations to employers.

We wrote this book because we saw a need to bring together some of the major thinking on self-assessment that would help guide job seekers through the job search maze. In so doing, we identify two different approaches that should assist you in clarifying what it is you do well, what you enjoy doing, and where you want to go. While each approach requires different investments of your time and energy and alternative ways of thinking about yourself, both approaches result in focusing your job search in directions that should please you. If followed properly, these approaches should put you on the road to finding the right job.

The pages that follow outline several options to discovering the right job for you. We do not offer a new approach to finding jobs nor any magical formulas for success. Rather, we attempt to clarify the best approaches to finding jobs that begin with *you*. In so doing, we analyze and synthesize numerous approaches we feel offer you the best alternatives.

Our emphasis throughout this book is on *options*. There are alternative ways to reaching the same destination, but you first need a roadmap that identifies your options before you can decide which way to go. If, for example, you need to better understand your interests and skills and how they relate to different jobs, we outline alternative ways of doing so, from self-directed pencil and paper exercises to professionally administered tests and computer software programs. If you feel you need additional assistance, we identify numerous other books and services that can help you. As such, this book should serve as a useful resource for finding what you need in the process of discovering the right job for you. It should also help you better define your destination.

We wish to thank the many career counselors who contributed both directly and indirectly to this book. It is their on-the-ground work and enthusiasm to make a difference in the lives of others that ultimately brings clarity to this subject as well as demonstrates the effectiveness of the approaches outlined in the following chapters. We especially owe a debt of gratitude to William J. Banis who collaborated with Ron in previous books in identifying the many self-assessment approaches appearing in this book. His contributions are especially evident in the chapters on identifying motivated abilities and skills and setting goals.

We wish you well in your search for the right job. But do us and yourself a favor: organize your thinking around doing first things first. Begin your job search by first examining who you are and where you want to go. Then take action based upon a clear objective. As you will discover in the following pages, the single-minded pursuit of an *objective* may be your greatest asset, regardless of the method you used to define your objective.

Whatever you do, get organized for what may become the greatest adventure of your life -- discovering the right job for you!

Ronald L. Krannich
Caryl Rae Krannich

Chapter One

DO FIRST THINGS FIRST

Most adults spend between 35 and 60 hours a week in work related activities. Some greet the Monday morning alarm cock with excitement and anticipation. Others dread the start of a new work week. Which are you or which will you become?

What do you want to do next month, next year, or even the rest of your life? Do you want a job that leads to major career advancement, more money, and greater power, or do you prefer less responsibility, less stress, and a slower pace? Perhaps you are primarily interested in pursuing a particular lifestyle centered around skills you most enjoy using? Do you want to work for someone else or run your own show? Where do you see your career and lifestyle 5, 10, or 20 years from now?

These questions lie at the heart of discovering the right job for you. They are the subject of this book. More important, they should become your central concerns as you develop a well organized and coherent plan for job success.

FINDING THE RIGHT JOB

Many people end up in the wrong jobs, because they fail to plan their careers around their major strengths and motivations. Not knowing what they do well and enjoy doing, they primarily seek jobs they think might be good for them in terms of salary and benefits. They seldom view jobs as being right for them in relation to their long-term patterns of interests, skills, and abilities. Once on the job, they may discover the job is an inappropriate *"fit"* for their abilities and motivational patterns. Salary and benefits become secondary considerations as they find few on-the-job rewards.

Few people are lucky enough to find jobs and pursue careers they really love. This is not to say most people are unhappy with their present jobs. Contrary to what many writers tell us -- that nearly 80 percent of the workforce is unhappy with their jobs -- annual national surveys continue to confirm that nearly 80 percent of today's workforce is relatively content with their present jobs. But could many of these people do much better if they used a different approach to finding jobs and advancing their careers?

> **The secret to discovering the right job for you is much more than an external search for "where the jobs are".**

Concerned with either keeping their present jobs or just finding one to pay the bills, most people seldom focus on the larger question of what job is really right for them. Instead, when looking for employment, they look **outside** themselves by focusing on *"where the jobs are"*. This approach leads them on a search for job vacancy announcements that look interesting to them rather than for jobs that may be right for them. They become preoccupied with fitting into the requirements of a job than with finding a job that is fit for them.

The secret to discovering the right job for you is much more than an external search for *"where the jobs are"*. It goes beyond the major initial approach of job seekers -- to quickly put together a resume so they can respond to vacancy announcements. While finding vacancy announcements and writing resumes are important elements in a job search, they should not be the first steps. They are not even the second or third things you need to do. They are intermediate activities that lie closer to the end of a job search.

At the very minimum, finding the right job for you begins with **you** -- knowing your interests, values, abilities, skills, motivations, and dreams. You must formulate this information on yourself into a powerful objective. This objective, in turn, provides the foundation for a well organized job search that will ultimately link your strengths and goals to the needs of employers.

Your first task should be to get to know yourself better in terms of where you have been going in the past, where you are at present, and where you wish to go in the future. By initially focusing on you rather than alternative job vacancies you feel you might be about to fit into, you begin building a sound basis for giving yourself positive career direction for many years to come.

This book is all about doing first things first. And the first thing you want to do is to answer the most important questions relating to your interests, values, abilities, skills, and objectives. In other words, you need to identify what it is you do well and enjoy doing *prior to* identifying where the jobs are and how to get one. The pages that follow show you how to best do this as you put yourself on a sound road to long-term career success.

A JOB FIT FOR YOU

Our major concern is that you find a job that is fit for you rather than one you think you might be able to fit into. This is an important distinction central to the remaining chapters in this book. Trying to *"fit into a job"* is the typical way most people find and keep jobs. They look for job vacancies and then try to stress those qualifications that will help them get the job. While some people find jobs they enjoy by using this approach, others are less fortunate. They often discover they are in the wrong job.

On the other hand, finding a job *"fit for you"* is what this book is all about. Our approach is based on a great deal of experience and common sense regarding how best to find and keep a job as well as advance a career. Time and again job seekers learn that it is more important to know what they want to do than to know where the job vacancies can be found. It's essential to know what you do well (abilities and skills), what you enjoy doing (interests and values), and what you want to do (objective) before writing each section of your resume or going for a job interview. If you do these first things first, you are more likely to find a job fit for you rather than one you may or may not fit into well.

GET ORGANIZED FOR SUCCESS

This book is all about doing first things first -- assessing your interests, abilities, and skills and formulating these into a powerful objective that will link you to the right job. This is not a book on *"what the jobs are"* or *"where the jobs are"* or even *"how to get a job"*. You will find numerous such books available today that primarily list alternative jobs and careers. Some of the best such books are identified in our bibliography (Chapter Fourteen) and in the order form at the end of this book. A few books attempt to identify the 100 or 200 *"hottest"* jobs and careers for the 1990s. Others are primarily directories of the most widely available jobs today. And still others attempt to show readers how to get into a few of today's best paying jobs.

> *Armed with this self knowledge, you will be in the best position to know what particular jobs and careers you should pursue.*

We focus on the important *linkage* between you and alternative jobs. Our approach begins and ends with you in reference to the job market. While you eventually need to research alternative jobs and careers (Chapter Eleven) as well as survey job vacancies, you first need to do what we outline in the first ten chapters -- discover what you do well and enjoy doing and what you want to do in the years ahead. Armed with this self knowledge, you will be in the best position to know what particular jobs and careers you should pursue. You will know that while some jobs may look interesting, they are inappropriate for your particular mix of interests and abilities. You will save a great deal of time and effort, avoid future disappointments, and enjoy what you will be doing in the future if you read this book prior to going on to finding a specific job you think might be good for you.

The chapters that follow are designed to easily walk you through the process of self discovery. After examining in Chapter Two your job search and skill needs, we examine in Chapter Three different approaches to finding a job. We conclude with advice on organizing a job search around the notion of doing *"first things first"* in the process of achieving job search success. Chapter Three is the critical overview chapter that shows you how all the job search pieces fit together as you face the task of organizing each step of your job search.

The remaining chapters take you step-by-step through the process of identifying your pattern of interests, values, abilities, skills, and motivations and then formulating them into a powerful job objective that will give your job search the necessary direction for success. Central to these chapters are two very different approaches to self-assessment and career direction. The first approach is widely practiced by a particular group of career counselors who believe in the power of predestination. It's based on both a deterministic and probabilistic theory of individual behavior -- your future performance will most likely be a repeat performance of your past patterns of behavior. Some career counselors also approach the subject from an explicit and somewhat controversial religious conviction: God has put his imprint on you and thus you cannot escape your fate; therefore, you need to discover what has ordained for you. This approach takes you down a narrow road where you are advised to be *"realistic"* about your future. An analysis of historical data on you -- rather than information on your future aspirations -- should determine where you will go in the future. By discovering your past patterns of motivated abilities and skills, you will be able to formulate realistic career goals as well as an appropriate job search action plan. Despite claims of effectiveness, doses of religious fundamentalism, and some hocus-pocus, most self-assessment devices using this approach are designed to reconstruct your history. We identify many of the most popular such devices and assess both their strengths and weaknesses.

The second approach is widely used in business -- primarily sales and entrepreneurship -- and in many religious circles. This is self-help psychological approach centered around such notions as *"self transformation"*, *"thinking big"*, *"following your dreams"*, *"positive thinking"*, *"you can be anything you want to be"*, and *"reach for the stars"*. It's the basic motivational approach used in such direct-sales operations as Amway, Shaklee, and Tupperware as well as in real estate and insurance; the popular wealth building approaches based on the self-motivational philosophies of Napolean Hill (**Think and Grow Rich**), Maltz Maxwell (**Psycho-Cybernetics**), Anthony Robbins (**Personal Power**),

David Schwartz (*The Magic of Thinking Big*), Claude Bristol (*The Magic of Believing*), Zig Ziglar (*How to Get What You Want*), Og Mandino (*Secrets of Success*) and many others; and the secular-religious writings of Dr. Norman Vincent Peale (*The Power of Positive Thinking*), Dr. Robert H. Schuller (*You Can Become the Person You Want to Be*), and Rabbi Harold Kushner (*When All You've Ever Wanted Isn't Enough*). Practitioners of this approach do not dwell on history. Indeed, one's history and past patterns of behavior are often seen as the *problem* rather the solution for charting a new future. These self-help philosophers see the past as an impediment -- something people need to break away from as they transform themselves and head in new directions. Being *"realistic"* is not a major concern, because realism is most likely a function of one's past patterns of behavior which are blinders to the future. These approaches stress the importance of setting high level -- even unrealistic -- goals and then developing the power to stay highly motivated and focused on those goals. Being single-minded in pursuing big goals is the basis for breaking out of past patterns as individuals embark on a new future.

At first glance these are radically different approaches that can produce very different outcomes for you. The first approach used by most career counselors is conservative, deterministic, probabilistic, and realistic. The second approach is radical, risky, and refreshing. Both face a fundamental dilemma when dealing with the future:

How can you chart your future if it is merely a reflection of your past or if it is based on a great deal of unrealistic big thinking?

The chapters that follow show how both approaches can best work for you. Each has certain strengths and weaknesses, and each works well for different people, depending on how they wish to chart their future. For some, the deterministic and probabilistic approach provides an excellent map for clarifying goals and organizing a well focused job search centering around one's major strengths. For others, who are interested in making major changes in their behavior, this approach is too limiting. We outline how they can best make changes without becoming captives of their pasts or frustrated by an inability to attain their aspirations.

WHERE DO YOU GO FROM HERE?

We wish you well as you take this journey into the wild and sometimes confusing world of self-discovery. While we are primarily concerned at this stage in taking you through the most critical initial stages of a job search, we also recognize the need to continue on through other important stages that result in meeting potential employers and receiving job offers. These other steps are outlined in our other books: *Careering and Re-Careering for the 1990s, High Impact Resumes and Letters, Dynamite Resumes, Dynamite Cover Letters, Interview for Success, Network Your Way to Job and Career Success,* and *Salary Success.* We also address particular job and career fields in the following books: *The Complete Guide to Public Employment, Find a Federal Job Fast, The Complete Guide to International Jobs and Careers, The Almanac of American Government Jobs and Careers, The Almanac of International Jobs and Careers,* and *The Educator's Guide to Alternative Jobs and Careers.* These and many other job search books are outlined in the final chapter of this book. They are available in many bookstores and libraries. For your convenience, they can also be ordered directly from Impact Publications by completing the order form at the end of this book or by acquiring a copy of the publisher's catalog.

Indeed, as a user of this book, you are entitled to a free copy of the most comprehensive career catalog available today -- *"Jobs and Careers for the 1990s".* To receive the latest edition of this catalog of over 1,000 annotated job and career resources, write to:

> IMPACT PUBLICATIONS
> ATTN: Job/Career Catalog
> 4580 Sunshine Court
> Woodbridge, VA 22192

They will send you a copy upon request. This 32-page catalog contains almost every important career and job finding resource available today, including many titles that are difficult if not impossible to find in bookstores and libraries. You will find everything from additional self-assessment books to books on resume writing, interviewing, government and international jobs, military, women, minorities, students, entrepreneurs as well as videos and computer software programs. This is an excellent resource for keeping in touch with the major resources that can assist you with every stage of your job search as well as with your future career development plans.

Chapter Two

IDENTIFY YOUR CAREERING COMPETENCIES

Doing first things first requires some basic self-knowledge about your capabilities to conduct an effective job search. Do you, for example, know what your major strengths are and how to communicate them to potential employers? Do you know which jobs are ideally suited for your particular skills and motivations? Can you develop a one to two-page resume that clearly communicates your qualifications to employers? How well can you plan and implement a job search that will lead to several interviews and a job offer that is right for you? We need to first address these questions prior to examining your interests, values, abilities, skills, motivations, and goals.

CAREERING COMPETENCIES

Knowing **where** the jobs are is important to your job search. But knowing **how to find a job** is even more important. Before you acquire names, addresses, and phone numbers of potential employers, you should possess the necessary job search knowledge and skills for gathering and using job information effectively.

Answers to many of your job related questions are found by examining your present level of job search knowledge and skills. Successful job seekers, for example, use a great deal of information as well as specific skills and strategies for getting the jobs they want.

Let's begin by testing for the level of job search information, skills, and strategies you currently possess as well as those you need to develop and improve. You can easily identify your level of job search competence by completing the following exercise:

TESTING YOUR CAREERING COMPETENCIES

INSTRUCTIONS: Respond to each statement by circling which number at the right best represents your situation.

SCALE:
1 = strongly agree
2 = agree
3 = maybe, not certain
4 = disagree
5 = strongly disagree

1. I know what motivates me to excel at work.   1 2 3 4 5

2. I can identify my strongest abilities and skills.   1 2 3 4 5

3. I have seven major achievements that clarify a pattern of interests and abilities that are relevant to my job and career.   1 2 3 4 5

4. I know what I both like and dislike in work.   1 2 3 4 5

5. I know what I want to do during the next 10 years.   1 2 3 4 5

6. I have a well defined career objective that focuses my job search on particular organizations and employers.   1 2 3 4 5

7. I know what skills I can offer employers in different occupations.   1 2 3 4 5

Identify Your Careering Competencies

8. I know what skills employers most seek in candidates.　　1 2 3 4 5

9. I can clearly explain to employers what I do well and enjoy doing.　　1 2 3 4 5

10. I can specify why an employer should hire me.　　1 2 3 4 5

11. I can gain support of family and friends for making a job or career change.　　1 2 3 4 5

12. I can find 10 to 20 hours a week to conduct a part-time job search.　　1 2 3 4 5

13. I have the financial ability to sustain a three-month job search.　　1 2 3 4 5

14. I can conduct library and interview research on difficult occupations, employers, organizations, and communities.　　1 2 3 4 5

15. I can write different types of effective resumes, job search letters, and thank-you notes.　　1 2 3 4 5

16. I can produce and distribute resumes and letters to the right people.　　1 2 3 4 5

17. I can list my major accomplishments in action terms.　　1 2 3 4 5

18. I can identify and target employees I want to interview.　　1 2 3 4 5

19. I can develop a job referral network.　　1 2 3 4 5

20. I can persuade others to join in forming a job search support group.　　1 2 3 4 5

21. I can prospect for job leads.　　1 2 3 4 5

22. I can use the telephone to develop prospects and
    get referrals and interview.   1 2 3 4 5

23. I can plan and implement an effective direct-mail
    job search campaign.   1 2 3 4 5

24. I can generate one job interview for every 10 job
    search contacts I make.   1 2 3 4 5

25. I can follow-up on job interviews.   1 2 3 4 5

26. I can negotiate a salary 10-20% above what an
    employer initially offers.   1 2 3 4 5

27. I can persuade an employer to renegotiate my
    salary after six months on the job.   1 2 3 4 5

28. I can create a position for myself in an organization.   1 2 3 4 5

                                           TOTALS   _____

                                      GRAND TOTAL   _____

ADDING IT UP

You can calculate your overall careering competencies by adding the numbers you circled for a composite scale. If your grand total is more than 75 points, you need to work on developing your careering skills. How you scored each item will indicate to what degree you need to work on improving specific job search skills. If your score is under 50 points, you are well on your way toward job search success. In either case, this book should help you better focus your job search as well as identify job search skills you need to acquire or strengthen.

Chapter Three

UNDERSTAND THE JOB FINDING PROCESS

Finding the right job requires that you (1) know who you are, (2) where you want to go, and (3) how to get there. This involves an important process of moving from an initial stage of self-awareness to several other action stages involving specific job search activities that eventually result in employment.

If you have a clear understanding of each element and relationship within this process, you should be in a better position to know who you are and where you want to go. By relating each element to the other, the process becomes a crucial blueprint revealing how to get where you want to go.

FINDING JOBS

If you are looking for your first job, reentering the job market after a lengthy absence, or planning a job or career change, you will join millions of individuals who do so each year. Indeed, more than 15 million people find themselves unemployed each year. Millions of others try to increase their satisfaction within the workplace as well as advance their careers by looking for alternative jobs and careers. If you are like most workers, you will make more than 10 job changes and between 3 and 5 career changes during your lifetime.

But how do you make such changes? Do you look for jobs in a well thought-out and planned manner or do new jobs come to you by accident? Most people make job or career transitions by accident. They do little other than take advantage of opportunities that may arise unexpectedly.

While chance and luck do play important roles in finding employment, we recommend that you *plan* for future job and career changes so that you will experience even greater degrees of chance and luck!

Finding a job or changing a career in a systematic and well-planned manner is hard yet rewarding work. The task should first be based on a clear understanding of the key ingredients that define jobs and careers. Starting with this understanding, you should next convert key concepts into action steps for implementing your job search.

> *A career is a series of related jobs which have common skill, interest, and motivational bases.*

A career is a series of related jobs which have common skill, interest, and motivational bases. You may change jobs several times without changing careers. But once you change skills, interests, and motivations, you change careers.

It's not easy to find a job given the present structure of the job market. You will find the job market to be relatively disorganized, although it projects an outward appearance of coherence. If you seek comprehensive, accurate, and timely job information, the job market will frustrate you with its poor communication. While you will find many employment services ready to assist you, such services tend to be fragmented and their performance is often disappointing. Job search methods are controversial and many are ineffective.

No system is organized to give people jobs. At best you will encounter a **decentralized and fragmented system** consisting of job listings in newspapers, trade journals, employment offices, or computerized job data banks -- all designed to link potential candidates with available job openings. Many people will try to sell you job information as well as questionable job search services, including testing and assessment exercises that you can easily do on your own with the help of this book! While efforts are underway to create a nationwide computerized job bank which would list available job vacancies on a daily basis, don't expect such data to become available soon nor to be very useful. Many of the listed jobs may be nonexistent, at a low skill and salary level, or represent only a few employers. In the end, most systems organized to help you find a job do not provide you with the information you need in order to land the job that is most related to your skills and interests.

> *Job finding skills are often more important to career success than job performance or work-content skills.*

THE CAREER DEVELOPMENT PROCESS

Finding a job is both an art and a science; it encompasses a variety of basic facts, principles, and skills which can be learned but which also must be adapted to individual situations. Thus, *learning how to find a job* can be as important to career success as *knowing how to perform a job.* Indeed, job finding skills are often more important to career success than job performance or work-content skills.

Our understanding of how to find jobs and change careers is illustrated on pages 16 and 17. As outlined on page 16, you should involve yourself in a four-step career development process as you prepare to move from one job to another.

Understand the Job Finding Process

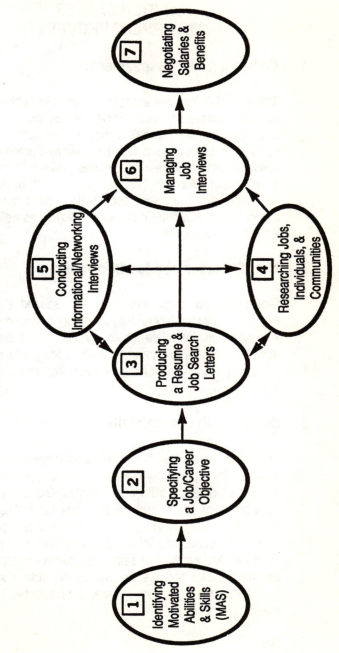

RELATIONSHIPS OF ACTIVITIES IN JOB SEARCH CAMPAIGN

1. Identifying Motivated Abilities & Skills (MAS)
2. Specifying a Job/Career Objective
3. Producing a Resume & Job Search Letters
4. Researching Jobs, Individuals, & Communities
5. Conducting Informational/Networking Interviews
6. Managing Job Interviews
7. Negotiating Salaries & Benefits

FOUR STEP CAREER DEVELOPMENT PROCESS

1. Conduct a self-assessment:

This first step involves assessing your skills, abilities, motivations, interests, values, temperaments, experience, and accomplishments -- the major concern of this book. Your basic strategy is to develop a firm foundation of information on *yourself* before proceeding to other stages in the career development process. This self-assessment develops the necessary self-awareness upon which you can effectively communicate your qualifications to employers as well as focus and build your career.

2. Gather career and job information:

Closely related to the first step, this second step is an exploratory, research phase of your career development. Here you need to formulate goals, gather information about alternative jobs and careers through reading and talking to informed people, and then narrow your alternatives to specific job targets.

3. Develop job search skills:

The third step focuses your career around specific job search skills for landing the job you want. As further outlined on page 17, these job search skills are closely related to one another as a series of *job search steps*. They involve conducting research, writing resumes and letters, prospecting and networking, conducting informational interviews, interviewing for a job, and negotiating salary and terms of employment. Each of these job search skills involves well-defined strategies and tactics you must learn in order to be effective in the job market.

4. Implement each job search step:

The final career development step emphasizes the importance of transforming understanding into *action*. You do this by implementing each job search step which already incorporates the knowledge, skills, and abilities you acquired in Steps 1, 2, and 3.

ORGANIZE AND SEQUENCE YOUR JOB SEARCH

The figure on page 17 further expands our career development process by examining the key elements in a successful job search. It consists of a seven-step process which relates your past, present, and future. The first two steps are outlined in this book. The remaining steps are examined in several of our other books that deal with resumes, letters, networking, interviews, and salary negotiations (see Chapter Fourteen).

Based on this concept, *your past* is well integrated into the process of finding a job or changing your career. Therefore, you should feel comfortable conducting your job search: it represents the best of what you are in terms of your past and present accomplishments as these relate to your present and future goals. If you base your job search on this process concept, you will communicate your *best self* to employers as well as focus on *your strengths* both during the job search and on the job.

Since the individual job search steps are interrelated, they should be followed in sequence. If you fail to properly complete the initial self-assessment steps, your job search may become haphazard, aimless, and costly. For example, you should never write a resume (Step 3) before first conducting an assessment of your skills (Step 1) and identifying your objective (Step 2). Relating Step 1 to Step 2 is especially critical to the successful implementation of all other job search steps. You *must* complete Steps 1 and 2 *before* continuing on to the other steps. Steps 3 to 6 may be conducted simultaneously because they complement and reinforce one another.

Try to sequence your job search as close to these steps as possible. The true value of this sequencing will become very apparent as you implement your plan.

The processes and steps identified on pages 16 and 17 represent the careering and re-careering processes we and others have used successfully with thousands of clients during the past 30 years. They are equally applicable to the job market of the 1990s as long as you recognize the importance of acquiring work-content skills along with job search skills. You must do much more than just know how to find a job. In the job markets of today and tomorrow, you need to constantly review your work-content skills to make sure they are appropriate for the changing job market. Once you have acquired the necessary skills through training and retraining, you will be ready to target your skills on particular jobs and careers that you do well and enjoy doing. You will be able to avoid the trap of trying to fit into jobs that are not conducive to your particular mix of interests, abilities, skills, and motivations.

Chapter Four

SEEK PROFESSIONAL ASSISTANCE WHEN NECESSARY

While some people can successfully conduct a job search based on the advice of books such as this, many others also need the assistance of various professional groups that offer specific career planning and job search services. These groups offer everything from testing and assessment services to offering contacts with potential employers, including job vacancy information and temporary employment services. Some do one-on-one career counseling while others sponsor one to three-day workshops or six to twelve-week courses on the various steps in the career planning process. You should know something about these services before you invest your time and money beyond this and other career planning and job search books.

OPTIONS

You have two options in organizing your job search. First, you can follow the principles and advice outlined in this and many other self-directed books. Just read the chapters and then put them into practice by following the step-by-step instructions. Second, you may wish to seek professional help to either supplement or replace this book. Indeed, many people will read parts of this book -- perhaps all of it -- and do nothing. Unwilling to take initiative, lacking sufficient time or motivation, or failing to follow-through, many people will eventually seek professional help to organize and implement their job search. They will pay good money to get someone else to tell them to follow the advice found in this book. Some people need this type of expensive motivation.

At the same time, we recognize the value of professional assistance. Especially with the critical assessment and objective setting steps (Chapters Six through Ten), some individuals may need more assistance than our advice and exercises provide. You may, for example, want to take a battery of tests to better understand your interests and values in relation to the workplace. And still others, due to a combination of job loss, failed relationships, or depression, may need therapy best provided by a trained psychologist or psychiatrist rather than career testing and information services provided by career counselors. If any of these situations pertain to you, by all means seek professional help.

POTENTIAL PITFALLS

You also should beware of pitfalls in seeking professional advice. While many services are excellent, other services are useless and fraudulent. Remember, career planning and job assistance are big businesses involving millions of dollars each year. Many people enter these businesses without expertise. Professional certification in these areas is extremely weak to nonexistent in some states. Indeed, many so-called *"professionals"* get into the business because they are unemployed. In other words, they major in their own problem! Others are frauds and hucksters who prey on vulnerable and naive people who feel they need a *"specialist"* or *"expert"* to get them a job. They will take your money in exchange for broken promises. You will find several services promising to assist you in finding all types of jobs. You should know something about these professional services before you venture beyond this book.

If you are interested in exploring the services of job specialists, begin by looking in the Yellow Pages of your telephone directory under these headings: Management Consultants, Employment, Resumes, Career Planning, and Social Services. Several career planning and employment services are available, ranging from highly generalized to very specific services. Most services claim they can help you. If you read this book, you will be in a better

Seek Professional Assistance When Necessary 23

position to seek out specific services as well as ask the right questions for screening the services. You may even discover you know more about finding a job than many of the so-called professionals!

While many services are excellent, other services are useless and fraudulent.

ALTERNATIVE SERVICES

At least 10 different career planning and employment services are available to assist you with your job search. Each has certain advantages and disadvantages. Approach them with caution. Never sign a contract before you read the fine print, get a second opinion, and talk to former clients about the **results** they achieved through the service. With these words of caution in mind, let's take a look at the variety of services available.

1. Public employment services:

Public employment services usually consist of a state agency which provides employment assistance as well as dispenses unemployment compensation benefits. Employment assistance largely consists of job listings and counseling services. However, counseling services often are a front to screen individuals for employers who list with the public employment agency. If you are looking for entry-level jobs in the $10,000 to $16,000 range, contact this service. Most employers do not list with this service, especially for positions paying more than $18,000 a year. If you walk through one of these offices, you will find that most people are unemployed and look poor; they will likely remain so for some time. In fact, some experts believe we should abolish these offices altogether because they exacerbate unemployment; they take people away from the more productive channels for employment -- personal contacts -- and put them in a line to waste time and meet few helpful and positive people.

2. Private employment agencies:

Private employment agencies work for money, either from applicants or employers. Approximately 8,000 such agencies operate nationwide. Many are highly specialized in technical, scientific, and financial fields. The majority of these firms serve the interests of employers since employers -- not applicants - represent repeat business. While employers normally pay the placement fee, many agencies charge applicants 10 to 15 percent of their first year salary. These firms have one major advantage: job leads which you may have difficulty uncovering elsewhere. Especially for highly specialized fields, a good firm can be extremely helpful. The major disadvantages are that they can be costly and the quality of the firms varies. Be careful in how you deal with them. Make sure you understand the fee structure and what they will do for you before you sign anything.

3. College/university placement offices:

College and university placement offices provide in-house career planning services for graduating students. While some give assistance to alumni, don't expect too much help if you already graduated. Many of these offices are understaffed or provide only rudimentary services, such as maintaining a career planning library, coordinating on-campus interviews for graduating seniors, and conducting workshops on how to write resumes and interview. Others provide a full range of well supported services including testing and one-on-one counseling. Indeed, many community colleges offer such services to members of the community on a walk-in basis. You can use their libraries and computerized career assessment programs, take personality and interest inventories, or attend special workshops or full-semester career planning courses which will take you through each step of the career planning and job search processes. You are well advised to enroll in such a course since it is likely to provide just enough structure and content to assess your motivated abilities and skills and to assist you in implementing a successful job search plan. Check with your local campus to see what services you might use.

4. Private career and job search firms:

Private career and job search firms help individuals acquire job search skills. They do not find you a job. In other words, they teach you much -- maybe more but possibly less -- of what is outlined in this book. Expect to pay anywhere from $1,500 to $10,000 for this service. If you need a structured environment for conducting your job search, contract with one of these firms. One of the most popular firms is Haldane Associates. Many of their pioneering career planning and job search methods are incorporated in this book. You will find branches of this nationwide firm in many major cities.

5. Executive search firms and headhunters:

Executive search firms work for employers in finding employees to fill critical positions in the $40,000 plus salary range. They also are called *"headhunters"*, *"management consultants"*, and *"executive recruiters"*. These firms play an important role in linking high level technical and managerial talent to organizations. Don't expect to contract for these services. Executive recruiters work for employers -- not applicants. If a friend or relative is in this business or you have relevant skills of interest to these firms, let them know you are available -- and ask for their advice. On the other hand, you may want to contact firms that specialize in recruiting individuals with your skill specialty. Several books identify how you can best approach *"headhunters"* on your own: ***How to Select and Use an Executive Search Firm*** (A. R. Taylor); ***How to Answer a Headhunter's Call*** (Robert H. Perry); ***The Headhunter Strategy*** (Kenneth J. Cole); ***The Directory of Executive Recruiters*** (Consultants News); and ***How to Get a Headhunter to Call*** (Howard S. Freedman).

6. Marketing services:

Marketing services represent an interesting combination of job search and executive search activities. They can cost $2,500 or more, and they work with individuals anticipating a starting salary of at least $40,000 but preferably over $60,000. These firms try to minimize the time and risk of applying for jobs. A typical operation begins with a client paying a $150 fee for developing psychological, skills, and interests profiles. Next, a marketing plan is outlined and a contract signed for specific services. Using word processing equipment, the firm normally develops a slick *"professional"* resume and mails it along with a cover letter, to hundreds -- maybe thousands -- of firms. Clients are then briefed and sent to interview with interested employers. While you can save money and achieve the same results on your own, these firms do have one major advantage. They save you *time* by doing most of the work for you. Again, approach these services with caution and with the knowledge that you can probably do just as well -- if not better -- on your own by following the step-by-step advice of this and other jobs search books.

7. Women's Centers and special career services:

Women's Centers and special career services have been established to respond to the employment needs of special groups. Women's Centers are particularly active in sponsoring career planning workshops and job information networks. These centers tend to be geared toward elementary job search activities, because their clientele largely consists of housewives who are entering or re-entering the workforce with little knowledge of the job market. Special career services arise at times for different categories of employees. For example, unemployed aerospace engineers, teachers, veterans, air traffic controllers, and government employees have formed special groups for developing job search skills and sharing job leads.

8. Testing and assessment centers:

Testing and assessment centers provide assistance for identifying vocational skills, interests, and objectives. Usually staffed by trained professionals, these centers administer several types of tests and charge from $300 to $800 per person. You may wish to use some of these services if you feel our activities in Chapters Six through Ten generate insufficient information on your skills and interests to formulate your job objective. If you use such services, make sure you are given one or both of the two most popular and reliable tests: **Myers-Briggs Type Indicator** and the **Strong-Campbell Interest Inventory.** You should find both tests helpful in better understanding your interests and decision-making styles. However, try our exercises before you hire a psychologist or visit a testing center. If you first complete these exercises, you will be in a better position to know exactly what you need from such centers. In many cases the career office at your local community college or women's center can administer these tests at minimum cost.

9. Job fairs or career conferences:

Job fairs or career conferences are organized by employment agencies to link applicants to employers. Usually consisting of one to two-day meetings in a hotel, employers meet with applicants as a group and on a one-to-one basis. Employers give presentations on their companies, resumes are circulated, and candidates are interviewed. Many of these conferences are organized to attract hard-to-recruit groups, such as engineers, computer programmers, and clerical and service workers. These are excellent sources for job leads and information -- if you get invited to the meeting or they are open to the public. Employers pay for this service -- not applicants.

10. Professional associations:

Professional associations often provide placement assistance. This usually consists of listing job vacancies and organizing a job information exchange at annual conferences. These meetings are good sources for making job contacts in different geographic locations within a particular professional field. But don't expect too much. Talking to people (networking) at professional conferences will probably yield better results than reading job listings and interviewing at conference placement centers.

CHOOSE THE BEST

Other types of career planning and employment services are growing and specializing in particular occupational fields. You may wish to use these services as a supplement to this book.

Whatever you do, proceed with caution, know exactly what you are getting into, and choose the best. Remember, there is no such thing as a free lunch, and you often get less than what you pay for. At the same time, the most

Seek Professional Assistance When Necessary

expensive services are not necessarily the best. Indeed, the free and inexpensive career planning services offered by many community colleges -- libraries, computerized career assessment programs, testing, and workshops - are often much superior to the other alternative services which can be expensive. After reading this book, you should be able to make intelligent decisions about what, when, where, and with what results you can use professional assistance. Shop around, compare services and costs, ask questions, talk to former clients, and read the fine print with your lawyer before giving an employment expert a job using your hard earned money!

Chapter Five

ALTERNATIVE CHOICES AND THE RIGHT "FIT"

Approaches to self-assessment are numerous and confusing. Everyone seems to offer their own unique theory, approach, test, or exercise purporting to provide insights into one's interests, values, skills, and abilities. For the uninitiated, this can be a bewildering experience as they attempt to acquire the most useful knowledge for directing their job search. Like the blind man feeling the trunk of an elephant, they're not sure what they have encountered. It could be an animal, but it might also be a tree.

Let's try to sort out the confusion by developing a clear idea of what we are doing and where we are going by addressing the key issues and questions involved in self-assessment. In so doing, you should be in a better position to determine which approaches will be most useful for your purposes.

ALTERNATIVE APPROACHES

You'll find numerous approaches to self-assessment. Some writers and career counselors claim you can do-it-on-your-own without the assistance of a professional. Indeed, some claim their self-directed exercises are just as valid as the testing instruments used by the professionals. Some claim they may even be superior to psychological testing. All you need to do is set aside

Alternative Choices and the Right "Fit"

a few hours of your time, complete the pencil and paper exercises, and analyze the information in reference to your particular job and career needs.

> *Your basic criteria for accepting an approach must be faith, common sense, and costs.*

While we have no way of knowing how valid the self-directed approach is in comparison to many validated testing instruments, the self-directed approach does claim testimonials from thousands of people who claim it worked for them. When considering whether to use a self-directed versus a testing approach to self-assessment, your basic criteria for accepting an approach must be faith, common sense, and costs. In other words, is it worth your time and effort to engage in these exercises? If it sounds and feels good and others say it works, try it out; they won't hurt you. Self-directed approaches will only cost you time. If you spend the necessary time to complete the exercises, chances are you will gain a great deal of useful information on yourself for directing your job search. And you may join thousands of others with a testimonial that the exercises really worked for you. Most job and career books that include a self-assessment section use some variety of this self-directed approach. One of the most intensive and elaborate such exercises is Richard Bolles' ***New Quick Job Hunting Map*** (Ten Speed Press). We will have more to say later about this and other self-directed exercises.

But not all self-directed approaches are the same. Some are simple listings or checklists of information about your feelings, ideas, relationships, or decision-making style. For example, identify the 10 things you most like about your job. Or prioritize from a list of 100 work values the 10 that best describe what's important to you. Others are more elaborate self-graded tests such as our careering competencies exercise in Chapter Two. And still others are complicated and extremely time consuming exercises that integrate facts and values into a system that analyzes several aspects of your job and career experiences. We'll share one of the most popular and useful such exercises with you in Chapter Eight when we integrate the simpler exercises of Chapters

Six and Seven into constructing a comprehensive picture of your major strengths.

BEWARE OF UNDERLYING ASSUMPTIONS

You should also be aware that underlying every approach is an implicit theory or set of assumptions about how you behave. When related to issues about your future, each approach may generate certain advice on how you should relate to the world of work.

Underlying every approach is an implicit theory or set of assumptions about how you behave.

The major theory underlying the most popular self-directed exercises is a combination of **historical determinism** and **probability**: your future behavior will largely be a reflection of your past patterns of behavior. The emphasis here is on **patterns** of behavior. In the most sophisticated form, these approaches direct you to identify your past patterns of motivated abilities and skills and then find jobs that will provide the best *"fit"* for your pattern. In the most extreme form, you will be told that you can't really do much about your patterns of behavior. They have been with you for years, and they will continue to dominate your behavior in the future. As this approach moves from description and explanation to prescription, it provides some sobering advice to those who believe in the power of self-transformation. Rather than try to change those patterns -- which you probably can't or won't do anyway -- it's best that you become more aware of them and learn to better live with yourself by seeking jobs and career opportunities that best utilize your *"strengths"*.

Not a bad theory for most people who are generally pleased to learn that they indeed have these patterns of motivated abilities and skills. Indeed, many people are elated to literally rediscover themselves after having completed exercises based on this theory. However, others are less enthusiastic after they learn the approaches largely generate information they already know about themselves.

Knowing your strengths is interesting descriptive and explanatory information about you, but it doesn't provide much prescriptive content about your future. For example, should you acquire new skills? What other jobs might be best suited for you? If you want to substantially increase your income, what should you do beyond what you have been doing in the past? Unfortunately, these self-directed exercises can give you little guidance about your future since they are based upon historical information about you.

> **Knowing your strengths is interesting descriptive and explanatory information about you, but it doesn't provide much prescriptive content about your future.**

When proponents of this approach attempt to address questions about the future, they get themselves in a real quagmire by dispensing questionable advice. The advice is usually the same and is part of the theory underlying the approach: follow your patterns. This is very conservative and unenlightening advice that is sometimes further justified with reference to such religious beliefs that God has established your pattern; therefore, you should learn to live with it and do the best you can within what is now your obvious limitations. There is little or no room in this approach for such notions as self-transformation -- breaking out of one's past patterns to embark on a new future. The clearest statements of this historical deterministic and probabilistic approach to self-assessment are found in **The Truth About You, What Color Is Your Parachute,** and **Where Do I Go From Here With My Life!** The approach is also implicit in the structure of **The Quick Job Hunting Map** and is found in a host of other literature and self-directed exercises associated with the works of Haldane, Holland, Bolles, Crystal, and their followers. With certain qualifications and revisions, this approach also occupies a major place in this book.

This is not to say these self-directed approaches do not work or are inherently deficit. Rather, they work well for thousands of people who embrace them and are willing to plan their futures around the notion of a pattern of motivated abilities and skills. Indeed, for 85 percent of the population, such an approach is very appropriate. They are not interested in self-transformation -- just get a better handle on their strengths and direct their lives accordingly. Our point is that like any approach, these approaches have limitations. They can only take you so far, depending on what you want to do with your life. If you already know your strengths but want to acquire new strengths that will take you into new job and career directions, you'll simply have to use other approaches that are less historical and more future in orientation. The most important approaches will deal with issues of change and self-transformation.

For 85 percent of the population, the self-directed approach is very appropriate.

A JOB TARGETED APPROACH

Another problem with many self-assessment approaches is that they help you generate self-understanding about your past interests, values, abilities, and skills, but they don't go to the next important step of linking that self-knowledge to specific jobs and careers most appropriate for your particular mix of skills or pattern of motivated abilities and skills. Indeed many people already know what they do well and enjoy doing, but they want to know what alternative jobs and careers are the most likely candidates for their experience. Many teachers, for example, know they have strong organization, communication, and supervision skills, but they don't know what types of jobs outside teaching might offer them better career opportunities, especially in terms of salaries and advancement.

Alternative Choices and the Right "Fit"

Our approach to self-assessment incorporates many of the previous approaches and then targets the self-assessment information toward alternative jobs and careers. In other words, you first need to know about your strengths through self-assessment and then relate those strengths to special jobs:

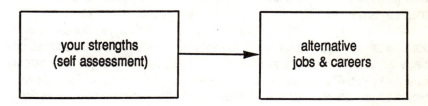

Once you know what jobs are likely to be the best *"fit"* for your particular mix of strengths, you will be well on the road to targeting your other job search activities (resumes, letters, networking, interviews) toward specific organizations, employers, and jobs.

ASK THE RIGHT QUESTIONS

We know that as much as 70 percent of the solution to most problems is found in first asking the right questions. In fact, you can easily reduce the complexity and confusion surrounding the many self-assessment approaches by focusing your attention on two basic questions:

1. *What do you do well?*

2. *What do you enjoy doing?*

The first question addresses your **skills and abilities.** The second question helps identify your **interests, values, and motivations.** Once you've answered these questions, you next need to link your skills and abilities (Question 1) with your interests, values, and motivations (Question 2). When integrated with each other, these elements become your **motivated abilities**

and skills (MAS). When examined through a series of self-assessment exercises, they become identified as your ***pattern*** of motivated abilities and skills (MAS pattern). This pattern becomes your unique set of job and career ***strengths*** that are best used in particular types of jobs.

What you ultimately need to do is find the best *"fit"* between your strengths (MAS pattern) and alternative jobs. You do this by first learning what your strengths are (self-assessment centered on identifying your MAS pattern) and then aligning them with different jobs that seem conducive to your strengths.

Put another way, this process involves five distinct yet closely related steps in the process of discovering the right job for you. These are outlined on page 37. A sixth step would involve restating your general job and career objective (Step 4) at a more specific level for the jobs you seek. This objective would appear on your resume. It would also be the focus for your networking activities as well as a subject to be elaborated upon during job interviews.

The remaining chapters examine each of these steps in the process of discovering the right job for you. In addition, we return to the issue of historical determinism versus self-transformation in Chapter Nine when we examine alternative approaches to self-assessment.

Alternative Choices and the Right "Fit" 37

FIND THE RIGHT JOB PROCESS

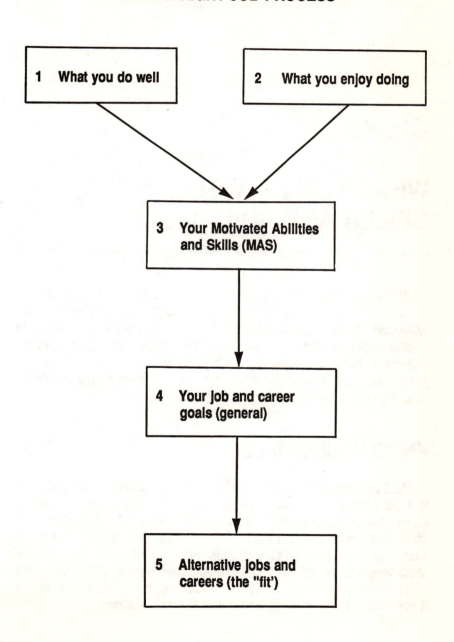

Chapter Six

WHAT YOU DO WELL: SKILLS AND ABILITIES

We live in a skills-based society where individuals market their skills to employers in exchange for money, position, and power. The ease by which individuals change jobs and careers is directly related to their ability to communicate their skills to employers and then transfer their skills to new work settings. To best position yourself in the job markets of today and tomorrow, you should pay particular attention to refining your present skills as well as acquiring new and more marketable skills.

KNOW YOUR SKILLS

But before you can refine your skills or acquire additional skills, you need to know what skills you presently possess. Unfortunately, few people can identify and talk about their skills even though they possess hundreds of skills which they use on a regular basis. This becomes a real problem when they must write a resume or go to a job interview. Since employers want to know about your specific abilities and skills, you must learn to both identify and communicate your skills to employers. You should be able to explain what it is you do well and give examples relevant to employers' needs.

What You Do Well: Skills and Abilities

What skills do you already have to offer employers? If you have just completed an educational program relevant to today's job market, the skills you have to offer are most likely related to the subject matter you studied. If you are changing jobs or careers, the skills you wish to communicate to employers will be those things you already have demonstrated you can do in specific jobs. They are your demonstrated abilities to accomplish work specific tasks.

TYPES OF SKILLS

Most people possess two types of skills that define their accomplishments and strengths as well as enable them to enter and advance within the job market:

- work-content skills

- functional skills

You need to acquaint yourself with these skills before communicating them to employers.

We assume you have already acquired certain **work-content skills** necessary to function effectively in today's job market. These *"hard skills"* are easy to recognize since they are often identified as *"qualifications"* for specific jobs; they are the subject of most educational and training programs. Work-content skills tend to be technical and job-specific in nature. Examples of such skills include proficiency in typing, programming computers, repairing air conditioners, or operating an X-ray machine. They may require formal training, are associated with specific trades or professions, are used only in certain job and career settings, and use a separate skills vocabulary, jargon, and subject matter for specifying technical qualifications for individuals entering and advancing in an occupation. While these skills do not transfer well from one occupation to another, they are critical for entering and advancing within certain occupations.

At the same time, you possess numerous **functional/transferable skills** employers readily seek along with your work-content skills. These *"soft skills"* are associated with numerous job settings, are mainly acquired through experience rather than formal training, and can be communicated through a general vocabulary. Functional/transferable skills are less easy to recognize since they tend to be linked to **dealing with processes** (communicating, problem-solving, motivating) rather than **doing things** (programming a computer, building a house, repairing air conditioners). While most people have only a few work-content skills, they have numerous -- perhaps as many as 300 -- functional/transferable skills. These skills enable job seekers to more easily change jobs. But you must first be aware of your functional skills before you can adequately relate them to the job market.

Most people view the world of work in traditional occupational job skill terms. This is a **structural view** of occupational realities. Occupational fields are seen as consisting of separate and distinct jobs which, in turn, require specific work-content skills. From this perspective, occupations and jobs are relatively self-contained entities. Social work, for example, is seen as being different from paralegal work; social workers, therefore, are not *"qualified"* to seek paralegal work.

Functional skills can be transferred from one job or career to another.

On the other hand, a **functional view** of occupations and jobs emphasizes similar characteristics among jobs as well as common linkages between different occupations. Although the structure of occupations and jobs may differ, they have similar functions. They involve working with people, data, processes, and objects. If you work with people, data, processes, and objects in one occupation, you can transfer that experience to other occupations which have similar functions. Once you understand how your skills relate to the functions as well as investigate the structure of different occupations, you should be prepared to make job changes from one occupational field to another. Whether you possess the necessary work-content skills to qualify for entry into the other occupational field is another question altogether.

The skills we identify and help you organize in this chapter are the functional skills career counselors normally emphasize when advising clients to assess their **strengths**. In contrast to work-content skills, functional skills

What You Do Well: Skills and Abilities

can be transferred from one job or career to another. They enable individuals to make some job and career changes without the need to acquire additional education and training. They constitute an important bridge for moving from one occupation to another.

Before you decide if you need more education or training, you should first assess both your functional and work-content skills to see how they can be transferred to other jobs and occupations. Once you do this, you should be better prepared to communicate your qualifications to employers with a rich skills-based vocabulary.

YOUR STRENGTHS

Regardless of what combination of work-content and functional skills you possess, a job search must begin with identifying your strengths. Without knowing these, your job search will lack content and focus. After all, your goal should be to find a job that is fit for you rather than one you think you might be able to fit into. Of course, you also want to find a job for which there is a demand. This particular focus requires a well-defined approach to identifying and communicating your skills to others. You can best do this by asking the right questions about your strengths and then conducting a systematic self-assessment of what you do best.

ASK THE RIGHT QUESTIONS

Knowing the right questions to ask will save you time and steer you into productive job search channels from the very beginning. Asking the wrong questions can cripple your job search efforts and leave you frustrated. The questions must be understood form the perspectives of both employers and applicants.

Two of the most humbling questions you will encounter in your job search are *"Why should I hire you?"* and *"What are your weaknesses?"* While employers may not directly ask these questions, feel assured they are asking them nonetheless. If these questions are not answered in a positive manner - directly, indirectly, verbally, or nonverbally -- your job search will likely flounder and you will join the ranks of the unsuccessful and disillusioned job searchers who feel something is wrong with them. Individuals who have lost their jobs are particularly vulnerable to these questions since many have lowered self-esteem and self-image as a result of the job loss. Many such people focus on what is wrong rather than what is right about themselves. Such thinking creates self-fulfilling prophecies and is self-destructive in the job market. By all means avoid such negative thinking.

Employers want to hire your value or strengths -- not your weaknesses.

Employers want to hire your *value or strengths* -- not your weaknesses. Since it is easier to identify and interpret weaknesses, employers look for indicators of your strengths by trying to identify your weaknesses. Your job is to communicate your strengths to employers. The more successful you are in doing this, the better off you will be in relation to both employers and fellow applicants.

Unfortunately, many people work against their own best interests. Not knowing their strengths, they market their weaknesses by first identifying job vacancies and then trying to fit their *"qualifications"* into job descriptions. This approach often frustrates applicants; it presents a picture of a job market which is not interested in the applicant's strengths. This leads some people toward acquiring new skills which they hope will be marketable, even though they do not enjoy using them. Millions of individuals find themselves in such misplaced situations. Your task is to avoid joining the ranks of the misplaced and unhappy work force by first understanding your skills and then relating them to your interests and goals. In so doing, you will be in a better position to target your job search toward jobs that should become especially rewarding and fulfilling.

FUNCTIONAL/TRANSFERABLE SKILLS

We know most people stumble into jobs by accident. Some are at the right place at the right time to take advantage of a job or career opportunity. Others work hard at trying to fit into jobs listed in classified ads, employment agencies, and personnel offices; identified through friends and acquaintances; or found by knocking on doors. After 15 to 20 years in the work world, many people wish they had better planned their careers from the very start. All of a sudden they are unhappily locked into jobs because of retirement benefits and the family responsibilities of raising children and meeting monthly mortgage payments.

After 10 or 20 years of work experience, most people have a good idea of what they don't like to do. While their values are more set than when they first began working, many people are still unclear as to what they do well and how their skills fit into the job market. What other jobs, for example, might they be qualified to perform? If they have the opportunity to change jobs or careers -- either voluntarily or forced through termination -- and find the time to plan the change, they can move into jobs and careers which fit their skills.

The key to understanding your non-technical strengths is to identify your transferable or functional skills. Once you have done this, you will be better prepared to identify what it is you want to do. Moreover, your self-image and self-esteem will improve. Better still, you will be prepared to communicate your strengths to others through a rich skills-based vocabulary. These outcomes are critically important for writing your resume and letters as well as for conducting informational and job interviews.

Let's illustrate the concept of functional/transferable skills by examining the case of educators. Many educators view their skills in strict work-content terms -- knowledge of a particular subject matter such as math, history, English, physics, or music. When looking outside education for employment, many educators seek jobs which will use their subject matter skills. However, they soon discover that non-educational institutions are not a ready market for such *"skills"*.

On the other hand, educators possess many other skills that are directly transferable to business and industry. Most educators are not aware of these skills and thus they fail to communicate their strengths to others. For example, research shows that graduate students in the humanities most frequently possess these transferable skills, in order of importance:

- critical thinking
- research techniques
- perseverance
- self-discipline
- insight
- writing
- general knowledge
- cultural perspective
- teaching ability
- self-confidence
- imagination
- leadership ability

Most functional/transferable skills can be classified into two general skills and trait categories -- organizational/interpersonal skills and personality/work-style traits:

TYPES OF TRANSFERABLE SKILLS

Organizational and Interpersonal Skills

___ communicating
___ problem solving
___ analyzing/assessing
___ planning
___ decision-making
___ innovating
___ thinking logically
___ evaluating
___ identifying problems
___ synthesizing
___ forecasting
___ tolerating ambiguity
___ motivating
___ leading
___ selling
___ performing
___ reviewing
___ attaining
___ team building
___ updating
___ coaching
___ supervising

___ trouble shooting
___ implementing
___ self-understanding
___ understanding
___ setting goals
___ conceptualizing
___ generalizing
___ managing time
___ creating
___ judging
___ controlling
___ organizing
___ persuading
___ encouraging
___ improving
___ designing
___ consulting
___ teaching
___ cultivating
___ advising
___ training
___ interpreting

What You Do Well: Skills and Abilities

___ estimating
___ negotiating
___ administering

___ achieving
___ reporting
___ managing

Personality and Work-Style Traits

___ diligent
___ patient
___ innovative
___ persistent
___ tactful
___ loyal
___ successful
___ versatile
___ enthusiastic
___ out-going
___ expressive
___ adaptable
___ democratic
___ resourceful
___ determining
___ creative
___ open
___ objective
___ warm
___ orderly
___ tolerant
___ frank
___ cooperative
___ dynamic
___ self-starter
___ precise
___ sophisticated
___ effective

___ honest
___ reliable
___ perceptive
___ assertive
___ sensitive
___ astute
___ risk taker
___ easy going
___ calm
___ flexible
___ competent
___ punctual
___ receptive
___ diplomatic
___ self-confident
___ tenacious
___ discrete
___ talented
___ empathic
___ tidy
___ candid
___ adventuresome
___ firm
___ sincere
___ initiator
___ competent
___ diplomatic
___ efficient

Use the following exercises to identify both your work-content and transferable skills. These self-assessment techniques stress your positives or strengths rather than identify your negatives or weaknesses. They should generate a rich vocabulary for communicating your *"qualifications"* to employers. Each exercise requires different investments of your time and effort as well as varying degrees of assistance from other people.

If you feel these exercises are inadequate for your needs, by all means seek professional assistance from a testing or assessment center staffed by a licensed psychologist. These centers do in-depth testing which goes further than these self-directed skill exercises.

CHECKLIST METHOD

This is the simplest method for identifying your strengths. Review the two types of transferable skills outlined on pages 44-45. Place a "1" in front of the skills that **strongly** characterize you; assign a "2" to those skills that describe you to a **large extent**; put a "3" before those that describe you to **some extent**. After completing this exercise, review the lists and rank order the 10 characteristics that best describe you on each list.

SKILLS MAP

Richard N. Bolles has produced two well-known exercises for identifying transferable skills based upon John Holland's typology of work environments. In his book, **The Three Boxes of Life** (Ten Speed Press), he develops a checklist of 100 transferable skills. They are organized into 12 categories or types of skills: using hands, body, words, senses, numbers, intuition, analytical thinking, creativity, helpfulness, artistic abilities, leadership, and follow-through.

Bolles' second exercise, *"The Quick Job Hunting Map"*, expands upon this first one. The *"Map"* is a checklist of 222 skills. This exercise requires you to identify seven of your most satisfying accomplishments, achievements, jobs, or roles. After writing a page about each experience, you relate each to the checklist of 222 skills. The *"Map"* should give you a comprehensive picture of what skills you (1) use most frequently, and (2) enjoy using in satisfying and successful settings. While this exercise may take six hours to complete, it yields an enormous amount of data on past strengths. Furthermore, the *"Map"* generates a rich skills vocabulary for communicating your strengths to others. The *"Map"* is found in the appendix of Bolles' **What Color Is Your Parachute?** (Ten Speed Press) or it can be purchased separately in beginning, advanced, or *"new"* versions from Ten Speed Press. His books as well as the latest version (1990) of his popular **New Quick Job Hunting Map** can be ordered directly from Impact Publications by completing the order information as the end of this book.

AUTOBIOGRAPHY OF ACCOMPLISHMENTS

Write a lengthy essay about your life accomplishments. This could range from 20 to 100 pages. After completing the essay, go through it page by page to identify what you most enjoyed doing (working with different kinds of information, people, and things) and what skills you used most frequently as well as enjoyed using. Finally, identify those skills you wish to continue using. After analyzing and synthesizing this data, you should have a relatively clear picture of your strongest skills.

COMPUTERIZED SKILLS ASSESSMENT SYSTEMS

While the previous self-directed exercises required you to either respond to checklists of skills or reconstruct and analyze your past job experiences, several computerized self-assessment programs are designed to help individuals identify their skills. Many of the programs are available in schools, colleges, and libraries. Some of the most widely used programs include:

- **Discover II**
- **Sigi-Plus**
- **Computerized Career Assessment and Planning Program**

These comprehensive career planning programs do much more than assess skills. As we will see in Chapter Eight, they also integrate other key components in the career planning process -- interests, goals, related jobs, college majors, education and training programs, and job search plans. These programs are widely available in schools, colleges, and libraries across the country. You might check with the career or counseling center at your local community college to see what computerized career assessment systems are available for your use. They are relatively easy to use and they generate a great deal of useful career planning information.

Chapter Seven

WHAT YOU ENJOY DOING: INTERESTS AND VALUES

Knowing what you do well is essential to understanding your strengths. However, knowing your abilities and skills alone does not necessarily give your job search the direction it needs for finding the right job. You also need to know your work values and interests. These are the basis for setting goals and motivating you to target your skills into certain job and career directions. The individual who types 120 words a minute, for example, possesses an excellent and highly marketable skill. But if the person doesn't enjoy using this skill and is more interested in working outdoors, this typing skill does not become a motivated skill nor is the individual likely to pursue a typing job. Your interests and values will determine whether or not certain skills should play a central role in your job search.

WORK INTERESTS

We all have interests. Some are related to jobs and careers whereas others relate to activities that define our hobbies and leisure activities. According to the *Guide to Occupational Exploration*, all jobs in the United States can be classified into 12 interest areas. Examine the following list of interest areas. In the first column check those work areas that appeal to you.

In the second column rank order those areas you checked in the first column. Start with "1" to indicate the most interesting:

YOUR WORK INTERESTS

Yes/No   **Ranking**   **Interest Area**
(x)   (1-12)

___   ___   **Artistic:** an interest in creative expression of feelings or ideas.

___   ___   **Scientific:** an interest in discovering, collecting, and analyzing information about the natural world, and in applying scientific research findings to problems in medicine, the life sciences, and the nature sciences.

___   ___   **Plants and animals:** an interest in working with plants and animals, usually outdoors.

___   ___   **Protective:** an interest in using authority to protect people and property.

___   ___   **Mechanical:** an interest in applying mechanical principles to practical situations by using machines or hand tools.

___   ___   **Industrial:** an interest in repetitive, concrete, organized activities done in a factory setting.

___   ___   **Business detail:** an interest in organized, clearly defined activities requiring accuracy and attention to details, primarily in an office setting.

___   ___   **Selling:** an interest in bringing others to a particular point of view by personal persuasion, using sales and promotion techniques.

What You Enjoy Doing: Interests and Values

___ ___ **Accommodating:** an interest in catering to the wishes and needs of others, usually on a one-to-one basis.

___ ___ **Humanitarian:** an interest in helping others with their mental, spiritual, social, physical, or vocational needs.

___ ___ **Leading and influencing:** an interest in leading and influencing others by using high-level verbal or numerical abilities.

___ ___ **Physical performing:** an interest in physical activities performed before an audience.

The *Guide for Occupational Exploration* also includes other checklists relating to home-based and leisure activities that may or may not relate to your work interests. If you are unclear about your work interests, you might want to consult these other interest exercises. You may discover that some of your home-based and leisure activity interests should become your work interests. Examples of such interests include:

LEISURE AND HOME-BASED INTERESTS

___ Acting in a play or amateur variety show.

___ Advising family members on their personal problems.

___ Announcing or emceeing a program.

___ Applying first aid in emergencies as a volunteer.

___ Building model airplanes, automobiles, or boats.

___ Building or repairing radio or television sets.

___ Buying large quantities of food or other products for an organization.

___ Campaigning for political candidates or issues.

___ Canning and preserving food.

___ Carving small wooden objects.

___ Coaching children or youth in sports activities.

___ Collecting experiments involving plants.

___ Conducting house-to-house or telephone surveys for a PTA or other organization.

___ Creating or styling hairdos for friends.

___ Designing your own greeting cards and writing original verses.

___ Developing film.

___ Doing impersonations.

___ Doing public speaking or debating.

___ Entertaining at parties or other events.

___ Helping conduct physical exercises for disabled people.

___ Making ceramic objects.

___ Modeling clothes for a fashion show.

___ Mounting and framing pictures.

What You Enjoy Doing: Interests and Values

___ Nursing sick pets.

___ Painting the interior or exterior of a home.

___ Playing a musical instrument.

___ Refinishing or re-upholstering furniture.

___ Repairing electrical household appliances.

___ Repairing the family car.

___ Repairing or assembling bicycles.

___ Repairing plumbing in the house.

___ Speaking on radio or television.

___ Taking photographs.

___ Teaching in Sunday School.

___ Tutoring pupils in school subjects.

___ Weaving rugs or making quilts.

___ Writing articles, stories, or plays.

___ Writing songs for club socials or amateur plays.

Indeed, many people turn hobbies or home activities into full-time jobs after deciding that such *"work"* is what they really enjoy doing.

Other popular exercises designed to identify your work interests include John Holland's *"The Self-Directed Search"* which is found in his book, **Making Vocational Choices: A Theory of Careers**. It is also published as a separate testing instrument, **The Self-Directed Search -- a Guide to Educational and**

Vocational Planning. Developed from Holland's Vocational Preference Inventory, this popular self-administered, self-scored, and self-interpreted inventory helps individuals quickly identify what type of work environment they are motivated to seek -- realistic, investigative, artistic, social, enterprising, or conventional -- and aligns these work environments with lists of common occupational titles. An easy exercise to use, it gives you a quick overview of your orientation toward different types of work settings that interest you.

Holland's self-directed search is also the basic framework used in developing Bolles' *"The Quick Job Hunting Map"* as found in his ***What Color Is Your Parachute*** and ***The New Quick Job Hunting Map*** books.

For more sophisticated treatments of work interests, which are also validated through testing procedures, contact a career counselor, women's center, or testing and assessment center for information on the following tests:

- Strong-Campbell Interest Inventory
- Myers-Briggs Type Indicator
- Edwards Personal Preference Schedule
- Kuder Occupational Interest Survey
- APTICOM
- Jackson Vocational Interest Survey
- Ramak Inventory
- Vocational Interest Inventory
- Career Assessment Inventory
- Temperament and Values Inventory

Numerous other job and career interest inventories are also available. For further information, contact a career counselor or consult Educational Testing Service which compiles such tests. ***The ETS Test Collection Catalog*** (New York: Oryx Press), which is available in many library reference sections, lists most of these tests. The ***Mental Measurements Yearbook*** (Lincoln, NE: University of Nebraska Press) also surveys many of the major testing and assessment instruments.

Keep in mind that not all testing and assessment instruments used by career counselors are equally valid for career planning purposes. While the Strong-Campbell Interest Inventory appears to be the most relevant for career decision-making, the Myers-Briggs Type Indicator has become extremely popular during the past two years. It is most useful for measuring individual

What You Enjoy Doing: Interests and Values 55

personality and decision-making styles than for predicting career choices. It is most widely used in pastoral counseling, student personnel, and business and religious organizations for measuring personality and decision-making styles. How these elements relate to career choices remains uncertain. In the meantime, many career counselors find Holland's **The Self-Directed Search** an excellent self-directed alternative to these professionally administered and interpreted tests.

WORK VALUES

Work values are those things you like to do. They give you pleasure and enjoyment. Most jobs involve a combination of likes and dislikes. By identifying what you both like and dislike about jobs, you should be able to better identify jobs that involve tasks that you will most enjoy.

Several exercises can help you identify your work values. First, identify what most satisfies you about work by completing the following exercise:

MY WORK VALUES

I prefer employment which enables me to:

___ contribute to society   ___ be creative

___ have contact with people   ___ supervise others

___ work alone   ___ work with details

___ work with a team   ___ gain recognition

___ compete with others   ___ acquire security

___ make decisions   ___ make a lot of money

___ work under pressure   ___ help others

___ use power and authority   ___ solve problems

____ acquire new knowledge   ____ take risks

____ be a recognized expert ____ work at my own pace

Select four work values from the above list which are the most important to you and list them in the space below. List any other work values (desired satisfactions) which were not listed above but are nonetheless important to you:

1. _____

2. _____

3. _____

4. _____

_____

_____

Another approach to identifying work values is outlined in the **Guide to Occupational Exploration.** If you feel you need to go beyond the above exercises, try this one. In the first column check those values that are most important to you. In the second column rank order the five most important values:

RANKING WORK VALUES

Yes/No Ranking   Work Values
 (x)   (1-5)

____   ____   **Adventure:** Working in a job that requires taking risks.

What You Enjoy Doing: Interests and Values

___ ___ **Authority:** Working in a job in which you use your position to control others.

___ ___ **Competition:** Working in a job in which you compete with others.

___ ___ **Creativity and self-expression:** Working in a job in which you use your imagination to find new ways to do or say something.

___ ___ **Flexible work schedule:** Working in a job in which you choose your hours to work.

___ ___ **Helping others:** Working in a job in which you provide direct services to persons with problems.

___ ___ **High salary:** Working in a job where many workers earn a large amount of money.

___ ___ **Independence:** Working in a job in which you decide for yourself what work to do and how to do it.

___ ___ **Influencing others:** Working in a job in which you influence the opinions of others or decisions of others.

___ ___ **Intellectual stimulation:** Working in a job which requires a great amount of thought and reasoning.

___ ___ **Leadership:** Working in a job which you direct, manage, or supervise the activities of others.

___ ___ **Outside work:** Working out-of-doors.

___ ___ **Persuading:** Working in a job in which you personally convince others to take certain actions.

___ ___ **Physical work:** Working in a job in which requires substantial physical activity.

___ ___ **Prestige:** Working in a job which gives you status and respect in the community.

___ ___ **Public attention:** Working in a job in which you attract immediate notice because of appearance or activity.

___ ___ **Public contact:** Working in a job in which you have day-to-day dealings with the public.

___ ___ **Recognition:** Working in a job in which you gain public notice.

___ ___ **Research work:** Working in a job in which you search for and discover new facts and develop ways to apply them.

___ ___ **Routine work:** Working in a job in which you follow established procedures requiring little change.

___ ___ **Seasonal work:** Working in a job in which you are employed only at certain times of the year.

___ ___ **Travel:** Working in a job in which you take frequent trips.

___ ___ **Variety:** Working in a job in which your duties change frequently.

___ ___ **Work with children:** Working in a job in which you teach or otherwise care for children.

___ ___ **Work with hands:** Working in a job in which you

What You Enjoy Doing: Interests and Values

                    use your hands or hand tools.

___ ___   **Work with machines or equipment:** Working in a job in which you use machines or equipment.

___ ___   **Work with numbers:** Working in a job in which you use mathematics or statistics.

Second, develop a comprehensive list of your past and present *job frustrations and dissatisfactions*. This should help you identify negative factors you should avoid in future jobs.

MY JOB FRUSTRATIONS AND DISSATISFACTIONS

List as well as rank order as many past and present things that frustrate or make you dissatisfied and unhappy in job situations:

                                                                     Rank

1. _____ ____

2. _____ ____

3. _____ ____

4. _____ ____

5. _____ ____

6. _____ ____

7. _____ ____

8. _____ ____

9. _____ ____

10. _____ ____

Third, brainstorm a list of *"Ten or More Things I Love to Do"*. Identify which ones could be incorporated into what kinds of work environments:

TEN OR MORE THINGS I LOVE TO DO

Item	Related Environment
1. _____	_____
2. _____	_____
3. _____	_____
4. _____	_____
5. _____	_____
6. _____	_____
7. _____	_____
8. _____	_____
9. _____	_____
10. _____	_____

Fourth, list at least ten things you most enjoy about work and rank each item accordingly:

What You Enjoy Doing: Interests and Values

```
┌──────── TEN THINGS I ENJOY THE MOST ────────┐
│                ABOUT WORK                   │
│                                             │
│                                        Rank │
│   1. _____    ___  │
│                                             │
│   2. _____    ___  │
│                                             │
│   3. _____    ___  │
│                                             │
│   4. _____    ___  │
│                                             │
│   5. _____    ___  │
│                                             │
│   6. _____    ___  │
│                                             │
│   7. _____    ___  │
│                                             │
│   8. _____    ___  │
│                                             │
│   9. _____    ___  │
│                                             │
│  10. _____    ___  │
│                                             │
└─────────────────────────────────────────────┘
```

    Fifth, you should also identify the types of interpersonal environments you **prefer working in.** Do this by specifying the types of people you like and dislike **associating with:**

INTERPERSONAL ENVIRONMENTS

**Characteristics of people   Characteristics of people
I like working with: I dislike working with:**

_____   _____

_____   _____

_____   _____

_____   _____

_____   _____

_____   _____

_____   _____

_____   _____

_____   _____

COMPUTERIZED SYSTEMS

Several computerized self-assessment programs are available that largely focus on career interests and values. The two major systems, *Discover II* and *Sigi-Plus*, include career interest segments. Some other popular systems are:

- *Career Interest Program*
- *Computerized Career Assessment and Planning Program*
- *Computerized Career Information System*
- *Values Auction Deluxe*

What You Enjoy Doing: Interests and Values　　　　　　　　　　　　　　　63

You should be able to get access to some of these and other related computer programs through your local community college, career center, or library.

YOUR FUTURE AS OBJECTIVES

All of these exercises are designed to explore your past and present work-related values. At the same time, you need to project your values into the **future**. What, for example, do you want to do over the next 10 to 20 years? We'll return to this type of value question when we address the critical objective setting stage of the job search process in Chapter Ten.

Chapter Eight

IDENTIFY YOUR MOTIVATED ABILITIES AND SKILLS (MAS)

Once you know what you do well and enjoy doing, you next need to analyze those interests, values, abilities, and skills that form a *recurring motivated pattern*. This pattern is the single most important piece of information you need to know about yourself in the whole self-assessment process. Knowing your skills and abilities alone without knowing how they relate to your interests and values will not give your job search the direction it needs for finding the right job.

WHAT'S YOUR MAS?

The concept of motivated abilities and skills (MAS) enables us to relate your interests and values to your skills and abilities. But how do we identify your MAS beyond the questions and exercises outlined thus far?

Your pattern of motivated abilities and skills becomes evident once you analyze your *achievements or accomplishments*. For it is your achievements that tell us what you both did well and enjoyed doing. If we analyze and synthesize many of your achievements, we are likely to identify a recurring pattern that most likely goes back to your childhood and which will continue to characterize your achievements in the future.

Identify Your Motivated Abilities and Skills (MAS)

Numerous self-directed exercises can assist you in identifying your pattern of motivated abilities and skills. The basic requirements for making these exercises work for you are time and analytical ability. You must spend a great deal of time detailing your achievements by looking at your past history of accomplishments. Once you have completed the historical reconstruction task, you must comb through your *"stories"* to identify recurring themes and patterns. This requires a high level of analytical ability which you may or may not possess. If analysis and synthesis are not two of your strong skills, you may need to seek assistance from a friend or professional who is good at analyzing and synthesizing information presented in narrative form. Career counseling firms such as Haldane Associates and People Management, Inc. are known for their use of this type of motivated pattern approach; they should be able to assist you.

Several paper and pencil exercises are designed to help identify your pattern of motivated abilities and skills. We outline some of the most popular and thorough such exercises that have proved useful to thousands of people.

THE SKILLS MAP

Richard Bolles' *"Quick Job Hunting Map"* has become a standard self-assessment tool for thousands of job seekers and career changers who are willing to spend the time and effort necessary for discovering their pattern of motivated abilities and skills. Offering a checklist of over 200 skills organized around John Holland's concept of *"The Self-Directed Search"* for defining work environments (realistic, investigative, artistic, social, enterprising, and conventional), the *"Map"* requires you to identify seven of your most satisfying accomplishments, achievements, jobs, or roles. After detailing each achievement, you analyze the details of each in relation to the checklist of skills. Once you do this for all seven achievements, you should generate a comprehensive picture of what skills you (1) use most frequently, and (2) enjoy using in satisfying and successful skills. This exercise not only yields an enormous about of information on your interests, values, skills, and abilities, it also assists you in the process of analyzing the data. If done property, the *"Map"* should also generate a rich *"Map"* vocabulary which you should use in your resumes and letters as well as in interviews.

The *"Map"* is available in different forms and for different levels of experience. The most popular versions are found in the Appendix of Bolles' *What Color Is Your Parachute?* and *The Three Boxes of Life* as well as in a separate publication entitled *The New Quick Job Hunting Map*. These three publications can be ordered directly from Impact Publications by completing the order information at the end of this book. The map is also available in three other versions: *The Beginning Quick Job-Hunting Map*, *How to Create a Picture of Your Ideal Job or Next Career*, and *The Classic Quick Job-Hunting Map*. These versions of the *"Map"* are most conveniently available directly from the publisher, Ten Speed Press (P.O. Box 7123, Berkeley, CA 94707).

We highly recommend using the Map because of the ease in which it can be used. If you will spend the six to twenty hours necessary to complete it properly, the *"Map"* will give you some important information about yourself. Unfortunately, many people become overwhelmed by the exercise and either decide not to complete it or they try to save time by not doing it according to the directions. You simply must follow the directions and spend the time and effort necessary if you want to get the maximum benefit from this exercise.

Keep in mind that like most self-assessment devices, there is nothing magical about the *"Map"*. Its basic organizing principles are simple. Like other exercises designed to uncover your pattern of motivated abilities and skills, this one is based on a theory of historical determinism and probability. In other words, once you uncover your pattern, get prepared to acknowledge it and live with it in the future.

AUTOBIOGRAPHY OF ACCOMPLISHMENTS

Less structured than the *"Map"* device, this exercise requires you to write a lengthy essay about your life accomplishments. Your essay may run anywhere from 20 to 200 pages. After completing it, go through it page by page to identify what you most enjoyed doing (working with different kinds of data, people, processes, and objects) and what skills you used most frequently as well as enjoyed using. Finally, identify those skills you wish to continue using. After analyzing and synthesizing this data, you should have a relatively clear picture of your strongest skills.

This exercise requires a great deal of self-discipline and analytic skill. To do it properly, you must write as much as possible, and in as much detail as possible, about your accomplishments. The richer the detail, the better will be your analysis.

MOTIVATED SKILLS EXERCISE

Our final exercise is one of the most complex and time consuming self-assessment exercises. However, it yields some of the best data on motivated abilities and skills, and it is especially useful for those who feel they need a more thorough analysis of their past achievements. This device is widely used by career counselors. Initially developed by Haldane Associates, this particular exercise is variously referred to as *"Success Factor Analysis", "System to Identify Motivated Skills",* or *"Intensive Skills Identification".*

This technique helps you identify which skills you *enjoy* using. While you can use this technique on your own, it is best to work with someone else. Since you will need six to eight hours to properly complete this exercise, divide your time into two or three work sessions.

The exercise consists of six steps. The steps follow the basic pattern of generating raw data, identifying patterns, analyzing the data through reduction techniques, and synthesizing the patterns into a transferable skills vocabulary. You need strong analytical skills to complete this exercise on your own. The six steps include:

1. **Identify 15-20 achievements:** These consist of things you enjoyed doing, believe you did well, and felt a sense of satisfaction, pride, or accomplishment in doing. You can see yourself performing at your best and enjoying your experiences when you analyze your achievements. This information reveals your motivations since it deals entirely with your voluntary behavior. In addition, it identifies what is right with you by focusing on your positives and strengths. Identify achievements throughout your life, beginning with your childhood. Your achievements should relate to specific experiences -- not general ones -- and may be drawn from work, leisure, education, military, or home life. Put each achievement at the top of a separate sheet of paper. For example, your achievements might appear as follows:

SAMPLE ACHIEVEMENT STATEMENTS

"When I was 10 years old, I started a small paper route and built it up to the largest in my district."

_____

"I started playing chess in ninth grade and earned the right to play first board on my high school chess team in my junior year."

_____

"Learned to play the piano and often played for church services while in high school."

_____

"Designed and constructed a dress for a 4-H demonstration project."

_____

"Although I was small compared to other guys, I made the first string on my high school football team."

_____

"I graduated from high school with honors even though I was very active in school clubs and had to work part-time."

_____

"I was the first in my family to go to college and one of the few from my high school. Worked part-time and summers. A real struggle, but I made it."

_____

"Earned an 'A' grade on my senior psychology project from a real tough professor."

"Finished my master's degree while working full-time and attending to my family responsibilities."

"Proposed a chef's course for junior high boys. Got it approved. Developed it into a very popular elective."

"Designed the plans for our house and had it constructed within budget."

2. **Prioritize your seven most significant achievements.**

```
┌─────── YOUR MOST SIGNIFICANT ───────┐
│             ACHIEVEMENTS            │
│                                     │
│   1. _____│
│                                     │
│   2. _____│
│                                     │
│   3. _____│
│                                     │
│   4. _____│
│                                     │
│   5. _____│
│                                     │
│   6. _____│
│                                     │
│   7. _____│
└─────────────────────────────────────┘
```

3. Write a full page on each of your prioritized achievements. You should describe:

- How you initially became involved.
- The details of *what you did* and *how you did it*.
- What was especially enjoyable or satisfying to you.

Use copies of the following form to outline your achievements.

DETAILING YOUR ACHIEVEMENTS

ACHIEVEMENT # __: _____
_____

1. **How did I initially become involved?** _____
_____
_____
_____

2. **What did I do?** _____
_____
_____
_____
_____
_____

3. **How did I do it?** _____
_____
_____

Identify Your Motivated Abilities and Skills (MAS)

```
_____
_____
_____

4. What was especially enjoyable about doing it?

_____
_____
_____
_____
_____
```

4. **Elaborate on your achievements:** Have one or two other people interview you. For each achievement have them note on a separate sheet of paper any terms used to reveal your skills, abilities, and personal qualities. To elaborate details, the interviewer(s) may ask:

   - *What was involved in the achievement?*
   - *What was your part?*
   - *What did you actually do?*
   - *How did you go about that?*

   Clarify any vague areas by providing an example or illustration of what you actually did. This interview should clarify the details of your activities by asking only *"what"* and *"how"* questions. Reproduce the following *"Strength Identification Interview"* form to guide you through this interview.

STRENGTH IDENTIFICATION INTERVIEW

Interviewee _____ **Interviewer** _____

INSTRUCTIONS: For each achievement experience, identify the *skills* and abilities which the achiever actually demonstrated. To obtain details of the experience, ask *what* was involved with the achievement and *how* the individual made the achievement happen. Avoid *"why"* questions which tend to mislead. Ask for examples or illustrations of what and how.

Achievement # ___   **Achievement #** ___   **Achievement #** ___

Recurring abilities and skills:

5. **Identify patterns by examining the interviewer's notes:** Together identify the recurring skills, abilities, and personal qualities *demonstrated* in your achievements. Search for patterns. Your skills pattern should be clear at this point; you should feel comfortable with it. If you have questions, review the data. If you disagree with a conclusion, disregard it. The results must accurately and honestly reflect how you operate.

6. **Synthesize the information by clustering similar skills into categories:** For example, your skills might be grouped in the following manner:

SYNTHESIZED SKILL CLUSTERS

Investigate/Survey/Read Inquire/Probe/Question	Teach/Train/Drill Perform/Show/Demonstrate
Learn/Memorize/Practice Evaluate/Appraise/Assess Compare	Construct/Assemble/Put Together
	Organize/Structure/Provide definition/Plan/Chart course Strategize/Coordinate
Influence/Involve/Get participation/Publicize Promote	
	Create/Design/Adapt/Modify

This exercise yields a relatively comprehensive inventory of your skills. The information will better enable you to use a *skills vocabulary* when identifying your objective, writing your resume and letters, and interviewing. Your self-confidence and self-esteem should increase accordingly.

OTHER ALTERNATIVES

Several other techniques also can help you identify your motivated abilities and skills:

1. List all of your hobbies and analyze what you do in each, which ones you like the most, what skills you use, and your accomplishments.

2. Conduct a job analysis by writing about your past jobs and identifying which skills you used in each job. Cluster the skills into related categories and prioritize them according to your preferences.

3. Purchase of copy of Arthur F. Miller and Ralph T. Mattson's *The Truth About You* and work through the exercises found in the Appendix. This is an abbreviated version of the authors' SIMA (System for Identifying Motivated Abilities) technique used by their career counseling firm, People Management, Inc. (10 Station Street, Simsbury, CT 06070). If you need professional assistance, contact this firm directly. They can provide you with several alternative services consistent with the career planning philosophy and approach outlined in this chapter.

4. Complete John Holland's *"The Self-Directed Search"*. You'll find it in his book, *Making Vocational Choices: A Theory of Careers* or in a separate publication entitled *The Self-Directed Search -- A Guide to Educational and Vocational Planning*.

BENEFIT FROM REDUNDANCY

The self-directed MAS exercises generate similar information. They identify interests, values, abilities, and skills you already possess. While aptitude and achievement tests may yield similar information, the self-directed exercises have three major advantages over the standardized tests: less expensive, self-

Identify Your Motivated Abilities and Skills (MAS)

monitored and evaluated, and measure motivation *and* ability.

Completing each exercise demands a different investment of your time. Writing your life history and completing the Motivated Skills Exercise as well as Bolles' *"Map"* are the most time consuming. On the other hand, Holland's self-directed search can be completed in a few minutes. But the more time you invest with each technique, the more useful information you will generate. We recommend creating redundancy by using at least two or three different techniques. This will help reinforce and confirm the validity of your observations and interpretations. If you are making a mid-career change and/or have a considerable amount of experience, we recommend using the more thorough exercises. The more you put into these techniques and exercises, the greater the benefit to other stages of your job search.

Chapter Nine

BEYOND SELF-KNOWLEDGE TO SELF-TRANSFORMATION

While most people may be content in identifying their motivated abilities and skills and pursuing jobs and careers that best fit their MAS patterns, other people desire to break out of past patterns as they embark on a new and uncharted future. For this latter group, identifying one's past patterns of motivated abilities and skills may be interesting self-knowledge, but it does not help put them on the road to jobs and careers that may, for example, pay more money or offer greater and more exciting challenges than in the past.

Take, for example, the clerk typist who can type 90 words a minute and enjoys working in pleasant surroundings and with mutually supportive individuals. After 10 years of thriving in this type of job where she has really enjoyed using her best skills and abilities, she decides that making $9.00 an hour is not her idea of a swell future; she's definitely not headed for the boardroom with her typewriter in hand! As her motivation (monitary needs) and career goals change, so too does her need for a different approach to finding a job and changing careers. Self-knowledge generated by the perspective and exercises found in Chapters Six, Seven, and Eight may be of limited usefulness as she seeks to break out of her past patterns of motivated abilities and skills.

FROM SELF-ASSESSMENT TO SELF-TRANSFORMATION

Motivation plays a central role in how and what we choose. When linked to aspirations and positive thinking, motivation can result in major changes in behavior which are largely unpredictable. This approach can and does result in major transformations for many people.

Underlining the concept of MAS is a very conservative notion that one's future behavior will largely be a reflection of one's past patterns of behavior. For some writers, this concept takes on very religious, even messianic, tones of predestination: God hath preordained your patterns when creating the *"unique you"*; therefore, you can't do much about these patterns other than better understand what they are and then better learn to live with them. This is an interesting and obviously controversial theory which also leads to a conservative view of where one can go from here with their life.

A form of historical determinism and probability, the MAS approach is probably valid for 85 percent of the workforce: past patterns of motivated abilities and skills are likely to recur in different work settings and situations; most people don't make significant departures from their basic patterns. In fact, most don't even try to make changes since they seem content at doing what they always do. However, this approach fails to assist individuals who are highly motivated to break out of their past patterns as they seek to embark on a new future. What, for example, can this approach do for the clerk typist who wishes to make $100,000 a year and no longer type?

Similar and rather simplistic theories of race and poverty have been used to explain why poor people are poor and are likely to stay poor in the future. Fortunately, we know better from experience.

People who are motivated to break out of their past patterns and create a new future need a different approach to jobs and careers. Indeed, self-knowledge based on traditional self-assessment exercises and tests may become an impediment to making future changes. Such information may constrain them from taking new actions that may result in major self-transformations.

CHANGE

Change based on breaking out of old patterns does indeed take place, and it happens more often than we think. And change often begins when an old mind set is replaced with a new one that rejects such simplistic notions of predestination. It begins when people reject old patterns of thinking, dream the impossible, imagine future states, or set seemingly unrealistic goals for themselves and remain motivated and persist in achieving their goals. A form of breakthrough thinking, this single-minded and determined thinking is demonstrated each year by thousands of people who break out of past patterns of behavior in a process of self-transformation. They make radical departures in their jobs and careers and go on to learning and developing new patterns of motivated abilities and skills. The approaches they use are instructive for our purposes.

Self knowledge based on traditional self-assessment exercises and tests may become an impediment to making future changes.

BREAKTHROUGH THINKING

The ability to make major changes in one's patterns of behavior as well as achieve new goals that may depart significantly from one's past experience is most closely associated with approaches to entrepreneurship and another school of religion. Such concepts as *"the power of positive thinking"*, *"thinking big"*, and *"shoot for the stars"* all have one central element in common -- breakthrough thinking centered around setting goals and then developing strategies for achieving those goals. Positive motivations and a *"can do"* attitude are the most important requirements for this approach. Individuals' goals need not be *"realistic"* since the notion of being realistic is based upon old patterns of behavior. Such approaches do not encourage individuals to engage in self-assessment. In fact, knowing a great deal about your past may be counterproductive since one of your past patterns might be an *"I can't do it"* attitude of *"realism"*. You may not be sufficiently unrealistic to be successful in whatever you do.

Positive motivations and a "can do" attitude are the most important requirements for this approach.

If you want to break out of your past as you seek to acquire a new future, you must approach jobs and careers from a different approach than identified in earlier chapters. Forget doing a self-assessment that directs you toward your past patterns. Instead, focus on your interests in relation to new objectives. Just set your goals, develop the proper mind set for achieving those goals, and work like the devil to attain those goals. In so doing, you'll have to maintain a positive attitude and a high level of motivation. Above all, you must persist, despite all odds and disappointments, until you achieve your goals.

THE ART OF BEING UNREALISTIC

This self-transformation approach has numerous and well respected practitioners. Anecdotal, intuitive, and creative in nature, it stresses the importance of **changing your behavior** rather than understanding your behavior. Indeed, the problem is often one's past patterns. The way to solve this problem is to create new patterns of thinking that will lead to success. The power to do this is found within each and every person -- the power to condition one's mind to think along new lines.

The techniques of self-transformation are as numerous as the practitioners of this approach. However, they all have some basic elements in common. Not only do they believe in the power of new thinking, but they chart similar strategies for achieving success:

- **Goals:** You must have clear idea of what you want to do. Get rid of negative thoughts, discard the *"I can't do it"* attitude, and stop procrastinating. You can do anything you want if only you first change your attitude and set high goals to strive for. Do not be constrained by your past when setting goals. Your past is likely to be an impediment to your future if you let it interfere with your goals.

- **Planning:** You must transform your goals into a series of action plans that detail how you will go about achieving the goals on a day-to-day basis. If you set goals without a corresponding plan for implementation, you may doom your *"big thinking"* to frustration and failure. A plan should outline incremental changes in your behavior each day. In the long run such a plan will help create a new *"unique you"*.

- **Discipline:** You must condition yourself to regularly take actions related to your goals and plans. Being single-minded in purpose and being persistent in what you do will be your greatest strengths in achieving your goals.

In the end, individuals are urged to make their behavior consistent with their goals. The mind should stay focused on goals since goals are the driving force for initiating change.

Essentially an individual decision-making approach, it is widely used in many circles to solve just about any problem that is defined as being within the power of individuals to tackle. This approach, for example, is used for:

- increasing personal wealth
- losing weight
- reorganizing personal finances
- motivating salespeople to increase sales

- generating more enthusiasm
- ending procrastination
- improving relationships

This is a personal form of snake-oil widely publicized by charismatic speakers who attempt to rouse the masses to take charge of their lives through positive and big thinking. It's the cure-all for almost any problem that you have the power to affect, and that includes almost every problem where you are involved.

> **The mind should stay focused on goals since goals are the driving force for initiating change.**

Once the major method used by a charismatic school of secular and religious positive thinkers who still dominate the growing *"success"* industry of books, videos, and audiocassettes, such as Napoleon Hill (***Think and Grow Rich***), Anthony Robbins (***Personal Power***), David Schwartz (***The Magic of Thinking Big***), Zig Ziglar (***How to Get What You Want***), Og Mandino (***Secrets of Success***), Dr. Norman Vincent Peale (***The Power of Positive Thinking***), and Dr. Robert H. Schuller (***You Can Become the Person You Want to Be***), today this approach is increasingly accepted and respected in business and government circles. Not only have many local insurance and real estate agents been raised on this approach in dealing with people, but many entrepreneurs have been motivated to leave established jobs and careers in pursuit of their business dreams. This approach has yet to make major inroads into career counseling circles where the deterministic and probabilistic MAS approach remains dominant.

What is especially interesting about this individual level problem-solving approach is its recent use as a problem-solving approach for organizations. Indeed, many businesses today use this approach to transform their operations in an increasingly competitive environment. Employees are urged to come up with new and innovative strategies and solutions to problems. Instead of analyzing the nature of problems and thus creating paralysis through analysis, they are encouraged to better define and clarify goals and then develop appropriate implementation strategies. An individual problem-solving approach has now come of age as an organizational problem-solving approach. As such, it has moved out of the hands of charismatic success advocates and into the portfolios of management consultants. As an approach to organizational change, this approach takes several forms:

- creative thinking
- brainstorming
- imagining and visualizing
- problem-solving
- breakthrough thinking
- self hypnosis

Research also shows that creative and intuitive people regularly use these methods for solving problems. The recent writings of Gerald Hadler and Shozo Hibino (*Breakthrough Thinking*) and William Fezler (*Creative Imagery*), which go beyond the anecdotal, have given this approach increased legitimacy for both individuals and organizations.

LEARNING NEW ABILITIES AND SKILLS

While the MAS approach to jobs and careers has little to say about education and training, since by definition the approach is aimed at uncovering past abilities and skills and then applying them to future jobs by focusing on *"transferable skills"*, the self-transformation approach recognizes the importance of acquiring new education and training as part of the process of self-transformation. Focusing on both goals and the future, the self-transformation approach deals with the issues of education and training relating to one's interests. If, for example, your new thinking specifies being a doctor or lawyer as a career goal, then you must incorporate medical or legal education, training, and certification in your plan of action. In other words, breaking out of your past patterns may mean going back to school where you will acquire new ways of thinking and doing things relevant to your goals.

NEVER SETTLE FOR YOUR PAST

One thing the self-transformation approach stresses in contrast to the MAS approach is that you should never settle for your past. You can make significant changes if you want to. But you must have clear goals and the necessary motivation to make the changes.

But for many people, change is not what they want. They are perfectly content at having their future be a reflection of their past MAS patterns. This is what gives their lives stability, predictability, and meaning. For them, the MAS approach is most appropriate. The self-transformation approach especially appeals to those who are risk takers and entrepreneurs.

Our point here is that your future need not be a reflection of your past. If you want more out of life, then you must use an approach that will move you from where you are at present to where you want to be in the future. How your future evolves will in part be determined by the approach you use to shaping that future. At the very least, the approach must outline a plan of action.

ACQUIRING MORE EDUCATION AND TRAINING

Do I have the necessary skills and experience required for the types of jobs that I'm interested in pursuing? How can I improve my present skill levels and acquire more experience? Do I need to learn new skills or be retrained for today's job market? Should I go back to school for a degree, diploma, or certificate? These questions are frequently asked by individuals first entering the job market or those making a job or career change. They will be central questions for individuals who use the self-transformation approach to planning their future.

It is difficult to provide simple answers to these questions. However, you first need to know what it is you want to do -- specify your goals. The next chapter (Ten) will assist you in doing this. Second, you must conduct research to identify what skills training is really required for particular positions. Notice, we say *skills training* -- not education. Although related, there is an important difference between skills training and education. Many employers are looking for specific skills rather than educational credentials. On the other hand, most educational institutions are still oriented toward transferring disciplines and subject matters to students rather than specific skills relevant to the world of work. If you fail to keep these two points in mind, you may waste a great deal of time and money on unnecessary training or seek jobs you are unqualified to perform.

> *You first need to know what it is you want to do.*

So how should you proceed? Do the necessary self-assessment and data gathering required to answer these questions. Begin by asking yourself a key question for orienting your job search:

"What do I really want to do?"

Once you have a clear idea of your job and career goals, you will be prepared to target your job search toward particular organizations, positions, and individuals.

Assuming you know what you want to do, your next step is to gather information to determine whether you possess the necessary skills to qualify for the job. Obviously, if you are a high school graduate wishing to become a medical doctor, engineer, lawyer, or accountant, you will need several years of highly specialized training for certification in these fields. However, if you want to become an FBI agent, just what educational background, experience, and demonstrated skills do you need? Where do you find this information?

You can begin answering these questions by consulting several publications as suggested in Chapter Eleven relevant to conducting a job search. Next, talk to individuals who have a working knowledge of the particular job or career you desire. Contact people in similar positions to what you are seeking. While many educators can be helpful, they should rank as a secondary information source. Few educators are objective sources for information about education and training requirements for particular jobs. Remember, most educators are relatively isolated from day-to-day job market realities. Furthermore, educators are in the business of keeping themselves employed by recruiting more students into existing programs as well as by developing new degree and certification programs. They literally *"stand where they sit"* by promoting more formal education, degrees, and certification -- whether or not such training and documentation is really necessary and relevant to the world of work.

> *Since many employers prefer conducting their own in-house training, they primarily look for individuals who are motivated, enthusiastic, trainable, and likeable.*

If you read materials and talk to informed individuals and employers, you will quickly learn what you need to do to be successful in your job search. If you learn you must return to school for a formal degree or certificate, your information sources will identify the most appropriate type of training you should acquire as well as recommend where best to receive the training. In many cases you will find you do not need additional training to qualify for a position. Since many employers prefer conducting their own in-house training, they primarily look for individuals who are motivated, enthusiastic, trainable, and likeable.

If you must acquire new skills, keep in mind several education and training options available to you:

- Public vocational education
- Private vocational education
- Employer training
- Apprenticeship programs
- Federal employment and training programs
- Armed Forces training
- Home study schools
- Community and junior colleges
- Colleges and universities

Most of these sources emphasize practical hands-on training. Private trade schools, for example, are flourishing while university enrollments are stagnant - indicating a shift to practical skills training in education. Each alternative has various advantages and disadvantages, and costs differ considerably.

1. Public vocational education:

Public vocational education is provided through secondary, postsecondary, and adult vocational and technical programs. The emphasis in many secondary schools is to give high school students vocational training in addition to the regular academic program. Postsecondary vocational education is provided for individuals who have left high school but who are not seeking a baccalaureate degree. Adult vocational and technical programs emphasize retraining or upgrading the skills of individuals in the labor force. The traditional agricultural, trade, and industrial emphasis of vocational education has been vastly expanded to include training in distribution, health, home economics, office, and technical occupations. Most programs train individuals for specific occupations, which are outlined in the *Occupational Outlook Handbook*. Each year over 20 million people enroll in public vocational education programs.

2. **Noncollegiate postsecondary vocational education:**

    Nearly 2 million people enroll in over 6,500 noncollegiate postsecondary schools with occupational programs each year. Most of these schools specialize in one of eight vocational areas: cosmetology/barber, business/commercial, trade, hospital, vocational/technical, allied health, arts/design, and technical. They offer programs in seven major areas: agribusiness, marketing and distribution, health, home economics, technical, business and office, and trade and industrial. Over 75 percent of these schools are privately owned institutions. And over 70 percent of the privately owned schools are either cosmetology/barber schools or business and commercial schools. Over 75 percent of the independent nonprofit schools are hospital schools. Over 1 million people complete occupational programs in noncollegiate postsecondary schools each year.

3. **Employer training:**

    Employers spend over $40 billion a year on in-house training and education programs. This training usually involves training new employees, improving employee performance, or preparing employees for new jobs. Skilled and semi-skilled workers are trained through apprenticeship programs, learning-by-doing, and structured on-the-job instruction. Structured classroom training is increasingly offered to skilled workers by in-house trainers, professional associations, private firms, or colleges and universities. Tuition-aid programs are used frequently among firms lacking in-house training capabilities.

4. Apprenticeship programs:

Apprenticeship programs normally range from one to six years, depending on the particular trade and organization. These programs are used most extensively in the trade occupations, especially in construction and metalworking. They involve planned on-the-job training in conjunction with classroom instruction and supervision. Over 500,000 individuals are involved in apprenticeship programs each year.

5. Federal employment and training programs:

Federal employment and training programs largely function through state and local governments. The major federal program is the Job Training Partnership Act (JTPA) program. Working through Private Industry Councils (PICs), the JTPA program is designed to train the economically disadvantaged as well as displaced workers who need assistance with skills training, job search, and job relocation. JTPA also operates two youth programs -- The Job Corps and the Summer Youth Employment Program. Other major Federal programs include two administered through the Employment and Training Administration: The Trade Adjustment Act program to assist workers displaced by foreign competition, and the Work Incentive (WIN) program for employable recipients of Aid to Families with Dependent Children, migrant and seasonal farm workers, Native Americans, and workers 55 and over.

6. Armed Forces Training:

The Armed Forces provide training in numerous occupational skills that may or may not be directly transferred to civilian occupations. Thousands of military recruits complete training programs in several transferable areas each year, such as computer repair, medical care, food service, metalworking, communications, and administration. Occupations unique to the military, such as infantry and guncrew, are less transferable to civilian occupations.

7. Home study (correspondence) schools:

Home study or correspondence schools provide a variety of training options. Most programs concentrate on acquiring a single skill; others may even offer a BA, MA, or Ph.D. by mail! Some programs are of questionable quality while others may be revolutionizing the education and training landscape of America. For many people, this is a convenient, inexpensive, and effective way to acquire new skills. Over 5 million people enroll in home study courses each year. Colleges and universities are quickly moving into the home study business by offering numerous televised courses for academic credit. The Public Broadcast System (PBS) offers several home study courses through its Adult Learning Service: computer literacy and applications, basic skills and personal enrichment, sales and customer service, effective communication skills, and management skills.

8. Community and junior colleges:

Community and junior colleges in recent years have broadened their missions from primarily preparing individuals for university degree programs to preparing them with skills for the job market. Accordingly, more of their programs emphasize vocational and occupational curriculums, such as data processing or dental hygiene, which are typically two-year programs resulting in an associate degree. Community and junior colleges will probably continue to expand their program offerings as they further adjust to the employment needs of communities. Nearly 5 million students enroll in community and junior college programs each year.

9. Colleges and universities:

Colleges and universities continue to provide the traditional four-year and graduate degree programs in various subject fields. While many of the fields are occupational-specific, such as engineering, law, medicine, and business, many other fields are not. The exact relationship of the degree program to the job market varies with different disciplines. As noted earlier, in recent years, graduates of many programs have had difficulty finding employment in their chosen fields. This is particularly true for students who only have a generalist background in the liberal arts. During the past decade many colleges and universities have adjusted to declining enrollments by offering several nontraditional occupational-related courses and programs. Continuing education, special skills training courses, short courses, evening course offerings, *"telecourses"*, and workshops and seminars on job-related matters have become popular with nontraditional, older students who seek specific skills training rather than degrees. At the same time, traditional academic programs are placing greater emphasis on internships and cooperative education programs in order to give students work experience related to their academic programs.

Additional training programs may be sponsored by local governments, professional associations, women's centers, YWCA's, and religious and civic groups. As training and retraining become more acceptable to the general public, we can expect different forms and types of training programs to be sponsored by various groups.

We also can expect a revolution in the training field, closely related to high-tech developments. Televised education and training courses should continue to increase in number and scope. Computer-based training, similar in some respects to traditional home study programs, will become more prevalent as computer software and interactive video training packages are developed in response to the new technology and the rising demand for skills training.

Individuals in tomorrow's education training markets will become examples of Toffler's *"prosumer society":* in a decentralized information market, individuals will choose what training they most desire as well as control when and where they will receive it. With the development of interactive video and computer training programs, individuals will manage the training process in a more efficient and effective manner than with the more centralized, time consuming, and expensive use of traditional student-teacher classroom instruction. This type of training may eventually make many of the previously discussed categories of education and training obsolete.

BECOME AN INFORMED CONSUMER

Several resources can help you decide which training path is more appropriate for you. If you use the *Discover II* computerized career planning system, you will find it includes a section that matches education and training programs with career interests. A few other computer software programs also match career interests with education and training programs. Contact your local secondary school, community college, or library for information on these programs.

You should begin your search for useful education and training information by consulting several useful publications. The major sources will be found in the reference section of libraries as well as in guidance offices and career planning centers of schools, colleges, universities, and specialized employment assistance centers. Most of these organizations maintain catalogues, directories, and files listing educational and training opportunities.

Two useful sources for information on education and training programs are *Peterson's Guides* and *Barron's Educational Series* which publish several excellent directories. Most of the directories are updated annually and include basic information on choosing programs and institutions best suited to your interests. Among the many titles offered by Peterson's and Barron's are:

- *Guide to Four-Year Colleges*
- *Guide to Two-Year Colleges*
- *The College Money Handbook*
- *Guides to Graduate Study:*
  -- *Graduate and Professional Programs*
  -- *Humanities and Social Sciences*

- -- Biological Agricultural and Health Sciences
- -- Physical Sciences and Mathematics
- -- Engineering and Applied Sciences
- *Regional Guides to Colleges*
  - -- Middle Atlantic
  - -- Midwest
  - -- New England
  - -- New York
  - -- Southeast
  - -- Southwest
  - -- West
- *Winning Money for College*
- *How to Write Your Way into College*
- *Job Opportunities for Engineering, Science, and Computer Graduates*
- *Job Opportunities for Business and Liberal Arts Graduates*
- *Guide to Medical and Dental Schools*
- *How to Prepare for the SAT*
- *Guide to Law Schools*
- *Profiles of American Colleges*
- *Guide to Graduate Business Schools*
- *Applying to Colleges and Universities in the United States*
- *Applying to Graduate School in the United States*
- *Competitive Colleges*
- *Colleges With Programs for Learning-Disabled Students*
- *National College Databank*
- *Handbook for College Admissions*
- *Guide to College Admissions*
- *How the Military Will Help You Pay for College*
- *Corporate Tuition Aid Programs*
- *Graduate Education Directory*

Most major libraries have copies of these publications in their reference section. If you cannot find them in your local library, check with your local bookstore or contact the publishers directly: Peterson's Guides, P.O. Box 2123, Princeton, NJ 08543-2123, Tel. 609/924/5338; and Barron's Educational Series, 250 Wireless Blvd., Hauppauge, NY 11788, Tel. 516/434-3311.

If you decide you need to acquire a specific skill, consult various professional or trade associations; many can provide you with a list of reputable institutions providing skills training in particular fields. The names, addresses, and telephone numbers of all major associations are listed in the **Encyclopedia of Associations** (Gale Publishers) and **National Trade and Professional Associations** (Columbia Books), two extremely useful directories found in the reference section of most libraries.

The U.S. Department of Labor's **Occupational Outlook Handbook** also lists useful names and addresses relating to employment training in specific fields. Consult the *"Where to Go For More Information"* section in the latest edition of this biannual directory. This book is also available in most libraries and can be purchased from Impact Publications by completing the order form at the end of this book.

For information on **private trade and technical schools**, be sure to contact the National Association of Trade and Technical Schools (NATTS). They produce three publications you may find useful: **Handbook of Accredited Private Trade and Technical Schools** and a series of pamphlets, including **How to Choose a Career and a Career School**. Write or call NATTS for information on these publications: NATTS, 2251 Wisconsin Ave., NW, Washington, DC 20007, Tel. 202/333-1021.

For information on **apprenticeship programs**, contact the Bureau of Apprenticeships and Training (BAT), U.S. Department of Labor, 200 Constitution Ave., NW, Washington, DC 20210, Tel. 202/535-0545. BAT offices are also found in each state. To find if there is a BAT office near you, consult the White Pages of your telephone directory under *"United States Government -- Department of Labor"*. Your local library and public employment service office should also have information on apprenticeship programs. For women interested in apprenticeship opportunities, send a self-addressed mailing label to the Women's Bureau, U.S. Department of Labor (200 Constitution Ave., NW, Washington, DC 20210, Tel. 202/523-6631) to receive a free copy of their useful publication, **A Woman's Guide to Apprenticeship**.

If you are interested in **home study and correspondence courses**, contact the National Home Study Council (NHSC) for information on home study programs. NHSC distributes copies of a useful publication entitled

Directory of Accredited Home Study Programs. For information on this and other NHSC publications, contact: National Home Study Council, 1601 18th St., NW, Washington, DC 20009, Tel. 202/234-5100.

You also need to determine the quality and suitability of these education and training programs. Many programs have reputations for fraud, abuse, and incompetence -- primarily take your time and money in exchange for broken promises. After all, this is a business transaction -- your money in exchange for their services. As an informed consumer, you must demand quality performance for your money. Therefore, when contacting a particular institution, ask to speak to former students and graduates. Write to the Council on Postsecondary Accreditation (One Dupont Circle, Suite 760, Washington, DC 20036) to inquire about the school's credentials. Focus your attention on the ***results*** or ***outcomes*** the institution achieves. Instead of asking how many faculty have Master or Ph.D. degrees, or how many students are enrolled, ask these performance questions:

- *What are last year's graduates doing today?*
- *Where do they work and for whom?*
- *How much do they earn?*
- *How many were placed in jobs through this institution?*

Institutions that can answer these questions focus on ***performance***. Beware of those that can't answer these questions, for they may not be doing an adequate job to meet your needs.

Most colleges and universities will provide assistance to adult learners. Contact student services, continuing education, academic advising, adult services, or women's offices at your local community college, college, or university. Be sure to talk to present and former students about the ***expectations and results*** of the programs for them. Always remember that educators are first in the business of keeping themselves employed and, second, in the business of delivering educational services. And today, more than ever, educational institutions need students to keep their programs alive. Don't necessarily expect professional educators to be objective about your future vis-a-vis their interests, skills, and programs. At the very least, you must do a critical evaluation of their programs and services.

If you need further assistance, contact a local branch of the National Center for Educational Brokering. While there is no national clearinghouse to help you match your goals with appropriate educational programs, NCEB can assist you nonetheless. NCEB counselors will help you identify your goals and career alternatives. For information on the center nearest you, contact the National Center for Educational Brokering, 329 9th St., San Francisco, CA 94103, Tel. 415/626-2378.

Other useful sources of information on education and training programs are your telephone book and employers. Look under *"Schools"* in the Yellow Pages of your telephone directory. Call the schools and ask them to send you literature and application forms and discuss the relevance of their programs to the job market. You should also talk to employers and individuals who have work experience in the field that interests you. Ask them how best to acquire the necessary skills for particular occupations. Most important, thoroughly research education and training alternatives before you invest any money, time, or effort.

> *Thoroughly research education and training alternatives before you invest any money, time, or effort.*

Beware of education and training myths. Additional education and training is not always the answer for entry or advancement within the job market. First, you should identify what it is you want to do and then identify what it is you need to do to get what you want. Indeed, employers spend over $40 billion each year on employee training and retraining -- much of which is spent because of the failure of traditional educational institutions. You may find it is best to get into a particular organization that provides excellent training for its employees. Most of the best run corporations rely on their own in-house training rather than on institutions outside the corporation. Even government is providing more and more training for its employees, although it still places a great deal of emphasis on formal educational credentials for entry into the government service.

Chapter Ten

SET GOALS AND STATE YOUR OBJECTIVE

Goals and objectives are statements of what you want to do in the future. When combined with an assessment of your interests, values, abilities and skills and targeted on specific jobs, they give your job search needed direction and meaning for the purpose of targeting specific employers. Without them, your job search may founder as you present a image of uncertainty and confusion to potential employers.

When you identify your strengths, you also create the necessary data base and vocabulary for developing your job objective. Using this vocabulary, you should be able to communicate to employers that you are a talented and purposeful individual who achieves **results**.

If you fail to do the preliminary self-assessment work necessary for developing a clear objective, you will probably wander aimlessly in the job market looking for interesting jobs you might fit into. Your goal, instead, should be to find a job or career that is compatible with your interests, motivations, skills, and talents as well as related to a vision of your future. In other words, try to find a job fit for you and your future rather than try to fit into a job that happens to be advertised and for which you think you can qualify.

EXAMINE YOUR PAST, PRESENT, AND FUTURE

Depending on how you approach your job search, your goals can be largely a restatement of your past MAS patterns or a vision of your future. If you base your job search on an analysis of your motivated abilities and skills, you may prefer restating your past patterns as your present and future goals. On the other hand, you may want to establish a vision of your future and set goals that motivate you to achieve that vision through a process of self-transformation.

The type of goals you choose to establish will involve different processes. However, the strongest goals will be those that combine your motivated abilities and skills with a realistic vision of your future.

ORIENT YOURSELF TOWARD THE NEEDS OF EMPLOYERS

Your objective should be a concise statement of what you want to do and what you have to offer to an employer. The position you seek is *"what you want to do"*; your qualifications are *"what you have to offer"*. Your objective should state your strongest qualifications for meeting employer's needs. It should communicate what you have to offer an employer without emphasizing what you expect the employer to do for you. In other words, your objective should be **work-centered,** not self-centered; it should not contain trite terms which emphasize what you want, such as give me a(n) *"opportunity for advancement"*, *"position working with people"*, *"progressive company"*, or *"creative position"*. Such terms are viewed as *"canned"* job search language which say little of value about you. Above all, your objective should reflect your honesty and integrity; it should not be *"hyped"*.

Identifying what it is you want to do can be one of the most difficult job search tasks. Indeed, most job hunters lack clear objectives. Many engage in a random, and somewhat mindless, search for jobs by identifying available job opportunities and then adjusting their skills and objectives to *"fit"* specific job openings. While you will get a job using this approach, you may be misplaced and unhappy with what you find. You will fit into a job rather than find a job that is fit for you.

Knowing what you want to do can have numerous benefits. First, you define the job market rather than let it define you. The inherent fragmentation and chaos of the job market should be advantageous for you, because it enables you to systematically organize job opportunities around your specific objectives and skills. Second, you will communicate professionalism to prospective employers. They will receive a precise indication of your interests, qualifications, and purposes, which places you ahead of most other applicants. Third, being purposeful means being able to communicate to employers what you want to do. Employers are not interested in hiring indecisive and confused individuals. They want to know what it is you can do for them. With a clear objective, based upon a thorough understanding of your motivated skills and interests, you can take control of the situation as you demonstrate your value to employers.

Finally, few employers really know what they want in a candidate. Like most job seekers, employers lack clear employment objectives and knowledge about how the job market operates. Thus, if you know what you want and can help the employer define his or her *"needs"* as your objective, you will have achieved a tremendously advantageous position in the job market.

BE PURPOSEFUL AND REALISTIC

Your objective should communicate that you are a ***purposeful individual who achieves results***. It can be stated over different time periods as well as at various levels of abstraction and specificity. You can identify short, intermediate, and long-range objectives and very general to very specific objectives. Whatever the case, it is best to know your prospective audience before deciding on the type of objective. Your objective should reflect your career interests as well as employers' needs.

Objectives also should be ***realistic***. You may want to become President of the United States or solve all the world's problems. However, these objectives are probably unrealistic. While they may represent your ideals and fantasies, you need to be more realistic in terms of what you can personally accomplish in the immediate future. What, for example, are you prepared to deliver to prospective employers over the next few months? While it is good to set challenging objectives, you can overdo it. Refine your objective by thinking about the next major step or two you would like to make in your career advancement -- not some grandiose leap outside reality!

> *Your objective should communicate that you are a purposeful individual who achieves results. It gives meaning and direction to all other activities.*

PROJECT YOURSELF INTO THE FUTURE

Even after identifying your abilities and skills, specifying an objective can be the most difficult and tedious step in the job search process; it can stall the resume writing process indefinitely. This simple one-sentence, 25-word statement can take days or weeks to formulate and clearly define. Yet, it must be specified prior to writing the resume and engaging in other job search steps. An objective gives meaning and direction to all other activities.

Your objective should be viewed as a function of several influences. Since you want to build upon your strengths and you want to be realistic, your abilities and skills will play a central role in formulating your work objective. At the same time, you do not want your objective to become a function solely of your past accomplishments and skills. You may be very skilled in certain areas, but you may not want to use these skills in the future. As a result, your values and interests filter which skills you will or will not incorporate into your work objective.

Overcoming the problem of historical determinism -- your future merely reflecting your past -- requires incorporating additional components into defining your objective. One of the most important is your ideals, fantasies, or dreams. Everyone engages in these, and sometimes they come true. Your ideals, fantasies, or dreams may include making $1,000,000 by age 45; owning a Mercedes-Benz and a Porsche; taking trips to Rio, Hong Kong, and Rome; owning your own business; developing financial independence; writing a best-selling novel; solving major social problems; or winning the Nobel Peace Prize. If your fantasies require more money than you are now making, you will need to incorporate monetary considerations into your work objective.

You can develop realistic objectives many different ways. We don't claim to have a new or magical formula, only one which has worked for many individuals. We assume you are capable of making intelligent career decisions if given sufficient data. Using redundancy once again, our approach is designed to provide you with sufficient corroborating data from several sources and perspectives so that you can make preliminary decisions. If you follow our steps in setting a realistic objective, you should be able to give your job search clear direction.

Four major steps are involved in developing a work objective. Each step can be implemented in a variety of ways:

STEP 1: Develop or obtain basic data on your functional/transferable skills, which we discussed in Chapter Six.

STEP 2: Acquire corroborating data about yourself from others, tests, and yourself. Several resources are available for this purpose:

    A.   **From others:** Ask three to five individuals whom you know well to evaluate you according to the questions in the *"Strength Evaluation"* form on page 101. Explain to these people that you believe their candid appraisal will help you gain a better understanding of your strengths and weaknesses from the perspectives of others. Make copies of this form and ask your evaluators to complete and return it to a designated third party who will share the information -- but not the respondent's name -- with you.

Set Goals and State Your Objective

STRENGTH EVALUATION

TO: _____

FROM: _____

 I am going through a career assessment process and thought you would be an appropriate person to ask for assistance. Would you please candidly respond to the questions below? Your comments will be given to me by the individual designed below; s/he will not reveal your name. Your comments will be used for advising purposes only. Thank you.

What are my strengths?

What weak areas might I need to improve?

In your opinion, what do I need in a job or career to make me satisfied?

Please return to: _____

B. From vocational tests: Although we prefer self-generated data, vocationally-oriented tests can help clarify, confirm, and translate your understanding of yourself into occupational directions. If you decide to use vocational tests, contact a professional career counselor who can administer and interpret the tests. We recommend several of the following tests:

- Strong-Campbell Interest Inventory
- Myers-Briggs Type Indicator
- Edwards Personal Preference Schedule
- Kuder Occupational Interest Survey
- APTICOM
- Jackson Vocational Interest Survey
- Ramak Inventory
- Vocational Interest Inventory
- Career Assessment Inventory
- Temperament and Values Inventory

C. From yourself: Numerous alternatives are available for you to practice redundancy. Refer to the exercises in Chapter Seven that assist you in identifying your work values, job frustrations and dissatisfactions, things you love to do, things you enjoy most about work, and your preferred interpersonal environments.

STEP 3: Project your values and preferences into the future by completing simulation and creative thinking exercises:

A. Ten Million Dollar Exercise: First, assume that you are given a $10,000,000 gift; now you don't have to work. Since the gift is restricted to your use only, you cannot give any part of it away. What will you do with your time! At first? Later on? Second, assume that you are given

Set Goals and State Your Objective 103

another $10,000,000, but this time you are required to give it all away. What kinds of causes, organizations, charities, etc. would you support? Complete the following form in which you answer these questions:

WHAT WILL I DO WITH TWO $10,000,000 GIFTS?

First gift is restricted to my use only:

_____

_____

_____

_____

Second gift must be given away:

_____

_____

_____

_____

SOURCE: John C. Crystal, *"Life/Work Planning Workshop"*

B. Obituary Exercise: Make a list of the most important things you would like to do or accomplish before you die. Two alternatives are available for doing this. First, make a list in response to this lead-in statement: *"Before I die, I want to..."*

---- **BEFORE I DIE, I WANT TO . . .** ----

1. _____

2. _____

3. _____

4. _____

5. _____

6. _____

7. _____

8. _____

9. _____

Set Goals and State Your Objective 105

10. _____

_____

Second, write a newspaper article which is actually your obituary for ten years from now. Stress your accomplishments over the coming ten year period.

―――――――― **MY OBITUARY** ――――――――

Obituary for Mr./Ms. _____ to appear in the _____ Newspaper in 2000.

C. **My Ideal Work Week:** Starting with Monday, place each day of the week on the headings of seven sheets of paper. Develop a daily calendar with 30-minute intervals, beginning at 7am and ending at mid-night. Your calendar should consist of a 118-hour week. Next, beginning at 7am on Monday (sheet one), identify the *ideal activities* you would enjoy doing, or need to do for each 30-minute segment during the day. Assume you are capable of doing anything; you have no constraints except those you impose on yourself. Furthermore, assume that your work schedule consists of 40 hours per week. How will you fill your time? Be specific.

— MY IDEAL WORK WEEK —

Monday

am		pm	
7:00	_____	4:00	_____
7:30	_____	4:30	_____
8:00	_____	5:00	_____
8:30	_____	5:30	_____
9:00	_____	6:00	_____
9:30	_____	6:30	_____
10:00	_____	7:00	_____
10:30	_____	7:30	_____
11:00	_____	8:00	_____
11:30	_____	8:30	_____
12:00	_____	9:00	_____
p.m.	_____	9:30	_____

Set Goals and State Your Objective 107

12:30 _____	10:00 _____
1:00 _____	10:30 _____
1:30 _____	11:00 _____
2:00 _____	11:30 _____
2:30 _____	12:00 _____
3:00 _____	Continue for Tuesday, Wednesday, Thursday, and Friday
3:30 _____	

D. My Ideal Job Description: Develop your ideal future job. Be sure you include:

- Specific interests you want to build into your job.
- Work responsibilities.
- Working conditions.
- Earnings and benefits.
- Interpersonal environment.
- Working circumstances, opportunities, and goals.

Use *"My Ideal Job Specifications"* on page 108 to outline your ideal job. After completing this exercise, synthesize the job and write a detailed paragraph which describes the kind of job you would most enjoy (use *"Description of My Ideal Job"* form on page 109):

MY IDEAL JOB SPECIFICATIONS

Job Interests	Work Responsibilities	Working Conditions	Earnings/ Benefits	Interpersonal Environment	Circumstances/ Opportunities/ Goals

```
┌──────── DESCRIPTION OF MY IDEAL JOB ────────┐
│                                              │
│  _____ │
│  _____ │
│  _____ │
│  _____ │
│  _____ │
│  _____ │
│  _____ │
│  _____ │
└──────────────────────────────────────────────┘
```

STEP 4: Test your objective against reality. Evaluate and refine it by conducting market research, a force field analysis, library research, and informational interviews.

A. Market Research: Four steps are involved in conducting this research:

1. **Products or services:** Based upon all other assessment activities, make a list of what you *do* or *make*:

```
┌──────── PRODUCTS/SERVICES ────────┐
│         I DO OR MAKE               │
│                                    │
│   1. _____  │
│   2. _____  │
│   3. _____  │
└────────────────────────────────────┘
```

```
┌─────────────────────────────────┐
│  4. _____ │
│  5. _____ │
│  6. _____ │
│  7. _____ │
│  8. _____ │
│  9. _____ │
│ 10. _____ │
└─────────────────────────────────┘
```

2. **Market:** Identify who needs, wants, or buys what you do or make. Be specific. Include individuals, groups, and organizations. Then, identify *what* specific *needs* your products or services fill. Next, assess the *results* you achieve with your products or services.

```
┌────── THE MARKET FOR MY ──────┐
│        PRODUCTS/SERVICES       │
│                                │
│ Individuals, groups, organizations needing me: │
│                                │
│  1. _____ │
│  2. _____ │
│  3. _____ │
│  4. _____ │
│  5. _____ │
│                                │
│ Needs I fulfill:               │
│                                │
│  1. _____ │
│  2. _____ │
└────────────────────────────────┘
```

Set Goals and State Your Objective 111

> 3. _____
> 4. _____
> 5. _____
>
> **Results/Outcomes/Impacts of my products/services:**
>
> 1. _____
> 2. _____
> 3. _____
> 4. _____
> 5. _____

3. **New Markets:** Brainstorm a list of *who else* needs your products or services. Think about ways of expanding your market. Next, list any new needs your current or new market has which you might be able to fill:

> **DEVELOPING NEW NEEDS**
>
> **Who else needs my products/services?**
>
> 1. _____
> 2. _____
> 3. _____
> 4. _____
> 5. _____

New ways to expand my market:

1. _____
2. _____
3. _____
4. _____
5. _____

New needs I should fulfill:

1. _____
2. _____
3. _____
4. _____
5. _____

4. **New products and/or services:** List any new products or services you can offer and any new needs you can satisfy:

NEW PRODUCTS/ SERVICES I CAN OFFER

1. _____
2. _____
3. _____
4. _____
5. _____

Set Goals and State Your Objective 113

```
┌─────── NEW NEEDS I CAN MEET ───────┐
│                                     │
│  1. _____ │
│                                     │
│  2. _____ │
│                                     │
│  3. _____ │
│                                     │
│  4. _____ │
│                                     │
│  5. _____ │
│                                     │
└─────────────────────────────────────┘
```

B. Force Field Analysis: Once you have developed a tentative or firm objective, force field analysis can help you understand the various internal and external forces affecting the achievement of your objective. Force field analysis follows a specific sequence of activities:

- Clearly state your objective or course of action.

- List the positive and negative forces affecting your objective. Specify the internal and external forces working *for* and *against* you in terms of who, what, where, when, and how much. Estimate the impact of each force upon your objective.

- Analyze the forces. Assess the importance of each force upon your objective and its probable affect upon you. Some forces may be irrelevant to your goal. You may need additional information to make a thorough analysis.

- Maximize positive forces and minimize negative ones. Identify actions you can take to strengthen positive forces and to neutralize, overcome, or reverse negative forces. Focus on the key forces which are real, important, and probable.

- Assess the feasibility of attaining your objective and, if necessary, modifying it in light of new information.

C. **Conduct Library Research:** This research should strengthen and clarify your objective. Consult various reference materials on alternative jobs and careers:

Career & Job Alternatives:	• *Dictionary of Occupational Titles* • *Encyclopedia of Careers & Vocational Guidance,* • *Guide for Occupational Exploration* • *Occupational Outlook Handbook* • *Occupational Outlook Quarterly*
Industrial Directories:	• *Bernard Klein's Guide to American Directories* • *Dun and Bradstreet's Middle Market Directory* • *Dun and Bradstreet's Million Dollar Directory* • *Encyclopedia of Business Information Sources* • *Geography Index* • *Poor's Register of Corporations, Directors,*

and Executives
- *Standard Directory of Advertisers*
- *The Standard Periodical Directory*
- *Standard and Poor's Industrial Index*
- *Standard Rate and Data Business Publications Directory*
- *Thomas' Register of American Manufacturers*

Associations:
- *Directory of Professional and Trade Associations*
- *Encyclopedia of Associations*

Government Sources:
- *The Book of the States*
- *Congressional Directory*
- *Congressional Staff Directory*
- *Congressional Yellow Book*
- *Federal Directory*
- *Federal Yellow Book*
- *Municipal Yearbook*
- *Taylor's Encyclopedia of Government Officials*
- *United National Yearbook*
- *United States Government Manual*
- *Washington Information Directory*

Newspapers:
- *The Wall Street Journal*
- Major city newspapers
- Trade newspapers
- Any city newspaper --

	especially the Sunday edition.
Business Publications:	• ***Barron's, Business Week, Business World, Forbes, Fortune, Harvard Business Review, Money, Time, Newsweek, U.S. News and World Report***
Other Library Resources:	• Trade journals (refer to the ***Directory of Special Libraries and Information Centers*** and ***Subject Collections: A Guide to Specialized Libraries of Businesses, Governments, and Associations***).
	• Publications of Chambers of Commerce; State Manufacturing Associations; and federal, state, and local government agencies
	• Telephone books -- The Yellow Pages
	• Trade books on *"How to get a job"*

4. **Conduct Informational Interviews:** This may be the most useful way to clarify and refine your objective. We'll discuss this procedure in the next chapter.

After completing these steps, you will have identified what it is you **can** do (abilities and skills), enlarged your thinking to include what it is you would **like** to do (aspirations), and probed the realities of implementing your objective. Thus, setting a realistic work objective is a function of the diverse considerations represented on page 118.

Your work objective is a function of both subjective and objective information as well as idealism and realism. We believe the strongest emphasis should be placed on your competencies and should include a broad data-base. Your work objective is realistic in that it is tempered by your past experiences, accomplishments, skills, and current research. An objective formulated in this manner permits you to think beyond your past experiences.

STATE A FUNCTIONAL OBJECTIVE

Your job objective should be oriented toward skills and results or outcomes. You can begin by stating a functional job objective at two different levels: a general objective and a specific one for communicating your qualifications to employers both on resumes and in interviews. Thus, this objective setting process sets the stage for other key job search activities. For the general objective, begin with the statement:

STATING YOUR GENERAL OBJECTIVE

I would like a job where I can use my ability to _____ which will result in _____ .

SOURCE: Richard Germann and Peter Arnold, **Bernard Haldane Associates Job & Career Building** (New York: Harper and Row, 1980), 54-55.

The objective in this statement is both a *skill* and an *outcome*. For example, you might state:

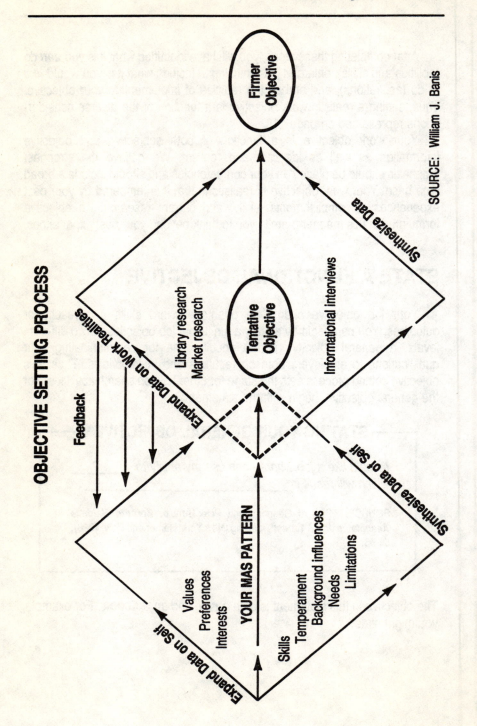

SKILLS-BASED AND RESULTS-ORIENTED OBJECTIVE

I would like a job where my experience in program development, supported by innovative decision-making and systems engineering abilities, will result in an expanded clientele and a more profitable organization.

At a second level you may wish to re-write this objective in order to target it at various consulting firms. For example, on your resume it becomes:

JOB TARGETED OBJECTIVE

An increasingly responsible research position in consulting, where proven decision-making and system engineering abilities will be used for improving organizational productivity.

The following are examples of weak and strong objective statements. Various styles are also presented:

WEAK OBJECTIVES

Management position which will use business administration degree and will provide opportunities for rapid advancement.

A position in social services which will allow me to work with people in a helping capacity.

A position in Personnel Administration with a progressive firm.

Sales Representative with opportunity for advancement.

STRONG OBJECTIVES

*To use computer science training in **software development** for designing and implementing operating systems.*

A public relations position which will maximize opportunities to develop and implement programs, to organize people and events, and to communicate positive ideas and images. Effective in public speaking and in managing a publicity/promotional campaign.

A position as a General Sales Representative with a pharmaceutical house which will use chemistry background and ability to work on a self-directed basis in managing a marketing territory.

A position in data analysis where skills in mathematics, computer programming, and deductive reasoning will contribute to new systems development.

Retail Management position which will use sales/customer service experience and creative abilities for product display and merchandising. Long term goal: Progression to merchandise manager with corporate-wide responsibilities for product line.

Responsible position in investment research and analysis. Interests and skills include securities analysis, financial planning, and portfolio management. Long range goal: to become a Chartered Financial Analyst.

Set Goals and State Your Objective

It is important to relate your objective to your audience. While you definitely want a good job, your audience wants to know what you can do for them. Remember, your objective should be work-centered, not self-centered.

Chapter Eleven

ALTERNATIVE JOBS AND CAREERS

Once you have a clear idea of what you do well and enjoy doing as well as what you would like to do in the future, you need to link this information on yourself to the world of work. For in the end, you need to know what jobs are most appropriate for someone with your *"qualifications"*. You do this through a combination of investigative techniques that put you close to real world of work and employers.

LINKAGE SYSTEMS

There are no magical formulas for relating information on yourself to specific jobs. While some employment specialists have attempted to develop elaborate systems that relate individual personality, interests, values, abilities, skills, and objectives to different job titles, most such efforts are highly generalized. At best they give you a general overview of the types of jobs you might be most interested in pursuing. Few provide you with the detailed information necessary for making informed career decisions.

Nonetheless, you should examine some of these systems for the purpose of narrowing your job choices to a manageable whole for further investigation. They come in many forms, from simple checklists for matching individual characteristics to job titles to more intensive forms of content analysis requiring a high level of analytical skills along with information on specific jobs. The U.S. Department of Labor, for example, has devised a job-matching chart that relates information on the individual to nearly 200 of the most popular and rapidly growing jobs in the United States. The jobs are clustered into related occupational areas as illustrated on pages 124-130. Further information on these and other related jobs is found in two of the Department of Labor's most widely used occupational reference works: **Occupational Outlook Handbook** and **Dictionary of Occupational Titles.** Both books are available through Impact Publications.

The **Guide for Occupational Exploration** also attempts to relate information on individuals to specific occupational fields. Focusing primarily on individual interests, but also including skills and abilities, the **Guide** identifies numerous jobs outlined to the **Dictionary of Occupational Titles** and relates these to information on individuals. This ambitious attempt to relate the descriptive nature of the **Dictionary** relevant to individual interests and skills provides a wealth of information on jobs. For individual occupations, it includes numerous checklists that help individuals focus on the interests, skills, abilities, and educational training required for each job.

Less ambitious and more eclectic systems are occasionally developed by enterprising writers and employment specialists. One of the most popular ones is outlined in Barry and Linda Gale's book, **Discover What You're Best At**. Dubbed the *"National Career Aptitude System"*, the author's so-called *"system"* is a series of self-administered multiple choice tests that examine business, clerical, logical, mechanical, numerical, and social aptitudes. These, in turn, are clustered and then related to some very general occupational titles. The book also includes brief descriptions of more than 1,100 careers which are also found in the **Dictionary of Occupational Titles** and the **Occupational Outlook Handbook.** The latest edition of this book assigns occupational cluster codes to each occupational description.

Practitioners of the motivated abilities and skills approach to career discovery also stress the importance of related self-assessment information to specific jobs. One of the most explicit and labor intensive approaches is outlined in Miller and Mattson's **The Truth About You.** Their analytical method, trademarked as the SIMA technique for assessing motivated abilities, is also used for *"matching"* one's motivated abilities with specific jobs. This requires identifying the motivational patterns associated with specific jobs and

DEPARTMENT OF LABOR JOB MATCHING SYSTEM*

Discover the Right Job For You!

	Job requirements								Work environment				Occupational characteristics			
	1. Leadership/persuasion	2. Helping/instructing others	3. Problem-solving/creativity	4. Initiative	5. Work as part of a team	6. Frequent public contact	7. Manual dexterity	8. Physical stamina	9. Hazardous	10. Outdoors	11. Confined	12. Geographically concentrated	13. Part-time	14. Earnings	15. Employment growth	16. Number of new jobs through 1995 (in thousands)	17. Entry requirements
Executive, Administrative, and Managerial Occupations																	
Managers and Administrators																	
Bank officers and managers	●	●	●	●	●	●						●		H	H	119	H
Health services managers	●	●	●	●	●	●								H	H	147	H
Hotel managers and assistants	●	●	●	●	●									¹	H	21	M
School principals and assistant principals	●	●	●	●	●									H	L	12	H
Management Support Occupations																	
Accountants and auditors		●	●		●	●						●		H	H	307	H
Construction and building inspectors		●	●	●	●			●		●				M	L	4	M
Inspectors and compliance officers, except construction		●	●	●	●			●		●				H	L	10	M
Personnel, training, and labor relations specialists	●	●	●	●	●									H	M	34	H
Purchasing agents	●		●		●									H	M	36	H
Underwriters		●												H	H	17	H
Wholesale and retail buyers	●	●	●	●	●									M	M	28	H
Engineers, Surveyors, and Architects																	
Architects		●	●	●	●	●								H	H	25	H
Surveyors	●			●		●	●			●				M	M	6	M
Engineers																	
Aerospace engineers		●	●	●								●		H	H	14	H
Chemical engineers		●	●	●										H	H	13	H
Civil engineers		●	●	●										H	H	46	H
Electrical and electronics engineers		●	●	●										H	H	206	H
Industrial engineers		●	●	●										H	H	37	H
Mechanical engineers		●	●	●										H	H	81	H
Metallurgical, ceramics, and materials engineers		●	●	●										H	H	4	H
Mining engineers		●	●	●										H	L	²	H
Nuclear engineers		●	●	●										H	L	1	H
Petroleum engineers		●	●	●									●	H	M	4	H
Natural Scientists and Mathematicians																	
Computer and Mathematical Occupations																	
Actuaries			●	●							●	●		H	H	4	H
Computer systems analysts	●	●	●	●								●		H	H	212	H
Mathematicians			●	●										H	M	4	H
Statisticians			●	●										H	M	4	H

¹ Estimates not available.
² Less than 500.

*Reprinted from the *Occupational Outlook Quarterly*, Fall 1986, U.S. Department of Labor Bureau of Labor Statistics.

Alternative Jobs and Careers

	1. Leadership/persuasion	2. Helping/instructing others	3. Problem-solving/creativity	4. Initiative	5. Work as part of a team	6. Frequent public contact	7. Manual dexterity	8. Physical stamina	9. Hazardous	10. Outdoors	11. Confined	12. Geographically concentrated	13. Part-time	14. Earnings	15. Employment growth	16. Number of new jobs through 1995 (in thousands)	17. Entry requirements
Physical Scientists			●	●										H	M		H
Chemists			●	●										H	L	9	H
Geologists and geophysicists			●	●	●					●		●		H	M	7	H
Meteorologists			●	●	●									H	M	1	H
Physicists and astronomers			●	●										H	L	2	H
Life Scientists																	
Agricultural scientists			●	●										¹	M	3	H
Biological scientists			●	●										H	M	10	H
Foresters and conservation scientists		●	●	●	●			●	●	●				H	L	2	H
Social Scientists, Social Workers, Religious Workers, and Lawyers																	
Lawyers	●	●	●	●	●	●								H	H	174	H
Social Scientists and Urban Planners																	
Economists			●	●										H	M	7	H
Psychologists		●	●	●		●								H	H	21	H
Sociologists			●	●		●								H	L	²	H
Urban and regional planners	●		●	●	●	●								H	L	2	H
Social and Recreation Workers																	
Social workers	●	●	●	●	●	●								M	H	75	H
Recreation workers	●	●	●	●	●	●	●	●		●			●	L	H	26	M
Religious Workers																	
Protestant ministers	●	●	●	●	●	●								L	¹	¹	H
Rabbis	●	●	●	●	●	●								H	¹	¹	H
Roman Catholic priests	●	●	●	●	●	●								L	¹	¹	H
Teachers, Counselors, Librarians, and Archivists																	
Kindergarten and elementary school teachers	●	●	●	●	●	●	●	●						M	H	281	H
Secondary school teachers	●	●	●	●	●	●		●						M	L	48	H
Adult and vocational education teachers	●	●	●	●	●	●	●	●					●	M	M	48	H
College and university faculty	●	●	●	●	●	●		●					●	H	L	−77	H
Counselors	●	●	●	●	●	●								M	M	29	H
Librarians	●	●	●	●	●	●		●					●	M	L	16	H
Archivists and curators			●	●	●									M	L	1	H
Health Diagnosing and Treating Practitioners																	
Chiropractors	●	●	●	●	●	●	●							H	H	9	H
Dentists	●	●	●	●	●	●	●							H	H	39	H
Optometrists	●	●	●	●	●	●	●							H	H	8	H
Physicians	●	●	●	●	●	●	●						●	H	H	109	H
Podiatrists	●	●	●	●	●	●	●							H	H	4	H
Veterinarians	●	●	●	●	●	●	●	●	●					H	H	9	H

¹ Estimates not available.
² Less than 500.

	Job requirements									Work environment				Occupational characteristics			
	1. Leadership/persuasion	2. Helping/instructing others	3. Problem-solving/creativity	4. Initiative	5. Work as part of a team	6. Frequent public contact	7. Manual dexterity	8. Physical stamina	9. Hazardous	10. Outdoors	11. Confined	12. Geographically concentrated	13. Part-time	14. Earnings	15. Employment growth	16. Number of new jobs through 1995 (in thousands)	17. Entry requirements
Registered Nurses, Pharmacists, Dietitians, Therapists, and Physician Assistants																	
Dietitians and nutritionists	•	•	•	•	•	•								M	H	12	H
Occupational therapists	•	•	•	•	•	•	•	•						¹	H	8	H
Pharmacists	•	•	•	•	•	•						•		H	L	15	H
Physical therapists	•	•	•	•	•	•	•	•						M	H	25	H
Physician assistants	•	•	•	•	•	•	•							M	H	10	M
Recreational therapists	•	•	•	•	•	•	•		•					M	H	4	M
Registered nurses	•	•	•	•	•	•	•	•	•				•	M	H	452	M
Respiratory therapists	•	•	•	•	•	•								M	H	11	L
Speech pathologists and audiologists	•	•	•	•	•	•								M	M	8	H
Health Technologists and Technicians																	
Clinical laboratory technologists and technicians		•		•		•					•			L	L	18	²
Dental hygienists		•			•	•	•	•					•	M	H	22	M
Dispensing opticians		•	•	•		•	•							M	H	10	M
Electrocardiograph technicians		•	•		•	•	•	•						¹	M	3	M
Electroencephalographic technologists and technicians		•	•		•	•	•	•						¹	H	1	M
Emergency medical technicians	•	•	•	•	•	•	•	•	•					L	L	3	M
Licensed practical nurses		•			•	•	•	•					•	L	M	106	M
Medical record technicians				•								•		L	H	10	M
Radiologic technologists		•			•	•	•		•					L	H	27	M
Surgical technicians		•			•	•	•							L	M	5	M
Writers, Artists, and Entertainers																	
Communications Occupations																	
Public relations specialists	•		•	•	•	•								H	H	30	H
Radio and television announcers and newscasters	•	•		•	•	•						•		L	M	6	H
Reporters and correspondents	•		•	•	•									¹	M	13	H
Writers and editors	•		•	•	•							•	•	¹	H	54	H
Visual Arts Occupations																	
Designers			•	•	•	•								H	H	46	H
Graphic and fine artists			•	•		•									H	60	M
Photographers and camera operators			•	•		•	•						•	M	H	29	M
Performing Arts Occupations																	
Actors, directors, and producers		•	•	•	•	•						•	•	L	H	11	M
Dancers and choreographers		•	•	•	•	•						•	•	L	H	2	M
Musicians			•	•	•	•						•	•	L	M	26	M

¹ Estimates not available.
² Vary, depending on job.

Alternative Jobs and Careers

	1. Leadership/persuasion	2. Helping/instructing others	3. Problem-solving/creativity	4. Initiative	5. Work as part of a team	6. Frequent public contact	7. Manual dexterity	8. Physical stamina	9. Hazardous	10. Outdoors	11. Confined	12. Geographically concentrated	13. Part-time	14. Earnings	15. Employment growth	16. Number of new jobs through 1995 (in thousands)	17. Entry requirements
Technologists and Technicians Except Health																	
Engineering and Science Technicians																	
Drafters					●		●					●		M	M	39	M
Electrical and electronics technicians			●		●	●	●							M	H	202	M
Engineering technicians			●		●	●	●							M	H	90	M
Science technicians			●		●		●							M	M	40	M
Other technicians																	
Air traffic controllers		●	●	●	●		●				●			H	L	¹	H
Broadcast technicians			●		●	●	●					●		M	H	5	M
Computer programmers			●	●								●		H	H	245	H
Legal assistants			²	●	²									M	H	51	L
Library technicians		●			●	●	●						●	L	L	4	L
Tool programmers, numerical control			●				●		●					M	H	3	M
Marketing and Sales Occupations																	
Cashiers		●			●	●						●	●	L	H	566	L
Insurance sales workers	●	●	●	●		●							●	M	L	34	M
Manufacturers' sales workers	●	●	●	●		●								H	L	51	H
Real estate agents and brokers	●	●	●	●		●					●		●	M	M	52	M
Retail sales workers	●	●		●		●							●	L	M	583	L
Securities and financial services sales workers	●	●	●	●		●							●	H	H	32	H
Travel agents	●	●	●	●		●								¹	H	32	M
Wholesale trade sales workers	●	●	●	●		●								M	H	369	M
Administrative Support Occupations, Including Clerical																	
Bank tellers					●	●						●	●	L	L	24	L
Bookkeepers and accounting clerks					●							●	●	L	L	118	L
Computer and peripheral equipment operators			●		●		●					●		L	H	143	M
Data entry keyers					●		●					●		L	L	10	L
Mail carriers						●	●	●		●				M	L	8	L
Postal clerks						●	●	●				●		M	L	−27	L
Receptionists and information clerks		●				●	●					●	●	L	M	83	L
Reservation and transportation ticket agents and travel clerks		●	●			●	●					●		M	L	7	L
Secretaries				●		●	●	●				L		L	L	268	L
Statistical clerks					●							●		L	L	−12	L
Stenographers					●		●	●	●					L	L	−96	L
Teacher aides	●	●				●	●	●	●				●	L	M	88	L
Telephone operators		●					●							L	M	89	L
Traffic, shipping, and receiving clerks				●	●	●								L	L	61	L
Typists							●					●	●	L	L	11	L

¹ Estimates not available.
² Less than 500.

Discover the Right Job For You!

Occupation	1	2	3	4	5	6	7	8	9	10	11	12	13	14	15	16	17
Service Occupations																	
Protective Service Occupations																	
Correction officers	●	●			●			●	●			●		M	H	45	L
Firefighting occupations		●	●		●	●	●	●	●				●	M	M	48	L
Guards					●	●	●	●	●			●	●	L	H	188	L
Police and detectives	●	●	●	●	●	●	●	●	●					M	M	66	L
Food and Beverage Preparation and Service Occupations																	
Bartenders			●		●	●	●				●		●	L	H	112	M
Chefs and cooks except short order			●			●	●				●		●	L	H	210	M
Waiters and waitresses			●		●	●	●						●	L	H	424	L
Health Service Occupations																	
Dental assistants		●			●	●	●						●	L	H	48	L
Medical assistants		●			●	●		●						L	H	79	L
Nursing aides		●			●	●	●	●					●	L	H	348	L
Psychiatric aides		●			●	●		●	●					L	L	5	L
Cleaning Service Occupations																	
Janitors and cleaners							●						●	L	M	443	L
Personal Service Occupations																	
Barbers					●	●	●				●		●	L	L	4	M
Childcare workers	●	●		●		●							●	L	L	55	L
Cosmetologists and related workers				●	●	●	●				●		●	L	H	150	M
Flight attendants		●			●	●	●	●						M	H	13	L
Agricultural, Forestry, and Fishing Occupations																	
Farm operators and managers	●	●	●	●	●		●	●		●				M	L	−62	L
Mechanics and Repairers																	
Vehicle and Mobile Equipment Mechanics and Repairers																	
Aircraft mechanics and engine specialists		●		●		●	●	●	●			●		H	M	18	M
Automotive and motorcycle mechanics		●				●	●	●	●		●			M	H	185	M
Automotive body repairers		●					●	●	●		●			M	M	32	M
Diesel mechanics		●				●	●	●	●		●			M	H	48	M
Farm equipment mechanics		●					●	●	●	●				M	L	2	M
Mobile heavy equipment mechanics		●					●	●	●		●			M	M	12	M

Alternative Jobs and Careers

	1	2	3	4	5	6	7	8	9	10	11	12	13	14	15	16	17
Electrical and Electronic Equipment Repairers																	
Commercial and electronic equipment repairers		●	●		●	●								L	M	8	M
Communications equipment mechanics		●	●		●	●								M	L	3	M
Computer service technicians		●	●		●	●								M	H	28	M
Electronic home entertainment equipment repairers		●	●		●	●		●				●		M	M	7	M
Home appliance and power tool repairers		●	●		●	●								L	M	9	M
Line installers and cable splicers		●		●		●	●	●	●					M	M	24	L
Telephone installers and repairers		●		●	●	●	●	●						M	L	−19	L
Other Mechanics and Repairers																	
General maintenance mechanics		●				●		●						M	M	137	M
Heating, air-conditioning, and refrigeration mechanics		●				●		●						M	M	29	M
Industrial machinery repairers		●				●	●	●						M	L	34	M
Millwrights		●				●		●						H	L	6	M
Musical instrument repairers and tuners						●								L	L	1	M
Office machine and cash register servicers			●	●	●	●								M	H	16	M
Vending machine servicers and repairers			●	●		●								¹	M	5	M
Construction and Extractive Occupations																	
Construction Occupations																	
Bricklayers and stonemasons		●		●		●	●	●	●					M	M	15	M
Carpenters		●		●		●	●	●	●					M	M	101	M
Carpet installers		●		●	●	●	●	●						M	M	11	M
Concrete masons and terrazzo workers		●		●		●	●	●	●					M	M	17	M
Drywall workers and lathers		●		●		●	●	●						M	M	11	M
Electricians		●		●		●	●	●	●					H	M	88	M
Glaziers		●		●		●	●	●	●					M	H	8	M
Insulation workers		●		●		●	●	●						M	M	7	M
Painters and paperhangers		●		●	●	●	●	●	●					M	L	17	M
Plasterers		●		●		●	●	●					●	M	L	1	M
Plumbers and pipefitters		●		●	●	●	●	●	●					H	M	61	M
Roofers		●		●		●	●	●	●					L	M	16	M
Sheet-metal workers		●		●		●	●	●						M	M	16	M
Structural and reinforcing metal workers		●		●		●	●	●	●					H	M	16	M
Tilesetters		●		●		●	●							M	M	3	M
Extractive Occupations																	
Roustabouts				●		●	●	●	●			●		M	L	²	L

¹ Estimates not available.
² Less than 500.

	1. Leadership/persuasion	2. Helping/instructing others	3. Problem-solving/creativity	4. Initiative	5. Work as part of a team	6. Frequent public contact	7. Manual dexterity	8. Physical stamina	9. Hazardous	10. Outdoors	11. Confined	12. Geographically concentrated	13. Part-time	14. Earnings	15. Employment growth	16. Number of new jobs through 1995 (in thousands)	17. Entry requirements
Production Occupations																	
Blue-collar worker supervisors	●	●	●	●	●		●		●					M	L	85	M
Precision Production Occupations																	
Boilermakers			●				●	●						M	L	4	M
Bookbinding workers		●			●		●	●	●		●			L	M	14	M
Butchers and meatcutters						●	●	●	●		●			L	L	−9	M
Compositors and typesetters							●	●	●		●			L	M	14	M
Dental laboratory technicians								●			●			L	M	10	M
Jewelers	●	●	●	●	●	●	●				●	●		L	L	3	M
Lithographic and photoengraving workers		●	●		●		●	●			●			H	M	13	M
Machinists			●				●	●	●		●			M	L	37	M
Photographic process workers							●				●			L	H	14	L
Shoe and leather workers and repairers		●			●	●	●							L	L	−8	M
Tool-and-die makers			●				●	●	●		●	●		H	L	16	M
Upholsterers							●	●			●			L	L	6	M
Plant and System Operators																	
Stationary engineers		●					●	●	●					M	L	4	M
Water and sewage treatment plant operators		●	●			●		●	●	●				L	M	10	M
Machine Operators, Tenders, and Setup Workers																	
Metalworking and plastic-working machine operators							●	●	●			●	●		L	3	L
Numerical-control machine-tool operators		●					●	●	●		●			M	H	17	M
Printing press operators	●	●		●			●	●	●		●			M	M	26	M
Fabricators, Assemblers, and Handworking Occupations																	
Precision assemblers			●				●	●			●			L	M	66	L
Transportation equipment painters							●	●	●		●			M	M	9	M
Welders and cutters							●	●	●	●				M	M	41	M
Transportation and Material Moving Occupations																	
Aircraft pilots			●	●	●		●					●		H	H	18	M
Busdrivers			●			●	●	●	●			●	●	M	M	77	M
Construction machinery operators				●			●	●	●	●	●			M	M	32	M
Industrial truck and tractor operators			●				●	●			●			M	L	−46	M
Truckdrivers			●				●	●			●			M	M	428	M
Handlers, Equipment Cleaners, Helpers, and Laborers																	
Construction trades helpers				●		●	●	●	●					L	L	27	L

then fitting one's individual motivational pattern with the most appropriate jobs. For example, if a motivational pattern for a specific sales position with XYZ computer company is oriented toward (1) working with technical details, (2) operating in a structured environment where team work is important, and (3) using one's ability to plan, initiate new contacts, and follow-up, and your particular motivational pattern indicates that these are the subject matters, circumstances, abilities, and operating relationships central to your work behavior, then you may have a ideal *"fit"* with this particular job. While this technique does not use tests and checklists, it does require a great deal of content analysis of content analysis relevant to special positions. Ideally, this type of analysis should be done on positions within specific organizations. As such, it requires a great deal of investigative work for uncovering the right job for you.

COMPUTER PROGRAMS

Several computerized programs provide information on jobs and careers appropriate for people with particular skill and interest profiles. The most popular, comprehensive, and powerful programs are the *Discover II* and *Sigi-Plus*. Both programs assist users in identifying their skills and interests and then matching them with appropriate jobs. Both programs are widely used in career and counseling centers at community colleges as well as four-year colleges and universities. Even if you are not a student, you should be able to get access to these programs through your local community college. You might also check with your local high school, women's center, or library for information on the availability of these excellent assessment programs.

Several other computerized job matching programs are also available. In particular, look for the following:

- *Computerized Career Assessment and Planning Program*
- *Computerized Career Information System*
- *The Micro Guide to Careers Series*

CONDUCT RESEARCH

We strongly recommend that you conduct research on jobs and organizations related to your MAS and objectives. This research can take different forms, from consulting key directories and reading books on alternative jobs to interviewing employees and potential employers in particular organizations. Your goal should be to get as much detailed information on jobs and organizations as possible. You want to know how particular jobs and employers relate to your MAS and objectives:

- *What types of people (personality, interests, skills) are best suited for each job?*

- *What type of environment do employees find themselves in?*

- *What appear to be the major requirements for success in this job?*

- *How are employees rewarded for their efforts?*

- *What kinds of relationships are employees expected to establish and maintain?*

Answers to these questions will help you determine whether particular jobs and organizations are appropriate *"fits"* given your MAS and objectives.

Your local library should be filled with useful job and career information for initial research. Reference and document rooms of libraries have some of the best career resources. Career planning offices at colleges and universities have a wealth of job and career information in their specialized libraries -- a wider selection than most general libraries.

You should start your research by examining several key directories that provide information on alternative jobs and careers:

- **The Occupational Outlook Handbook** (U.S. Department of Labor). This massive directory is the *"bible"* for identifying over 20,000 job titles. Each job is annotated, organized by major job categories, and cross-referenced by industry and title.

Alternative Jobs and Careers

- ***Occupational Outlook Handbook*** (U.S. Department of Labor). Published biannually, this is the standard sourcebook on over 200 of America's most popular careers. Provides clear descriptions of each job, including working conditions, educational and training requirements, salaries, and future prospects.

- ***Encyclopedia of Careers and Vocational Guidance***, 4 Volumes (J. G. Ferguson Co.). Newly revised (1990) this standard reference examines hundreds of technical and high-tech occupations in addition to the standard career and job fields. Vol 1: *Industry Profiles*; Vol. 2: *Professional Careers*; Vol. 3: *Specific and General Careers*; Vol. 4: *Technicians Careers.*

- ***The Guide for Occupational Exploration*** (National Forum Foundation). Based on the U.S. Department of Labor research, this guide lists more than 20,000 jobs by occupational cluster, skills required, job title, and industry groups. This is the key book that provides some analytical substance to the ***Dictionary of Occupational Titles*** and the ***Occupational Outlook Handbook.***

You will also find several books that focus on alternative jobs and careers. National Textbook Company, for example, publishes one of the most comprehensive series of books on alternative jobs and careers. Their books now address 138 different job and career fields. Representative titles in their *"Opportunities in..."* series include:

- ***Opportunities in Advertising***
- ***Opportunities in Airline Careers***
- ***Opportunities in Banking***
- ***Opportunities in Business Management***
- ***Opportunities in Child Care***
- ***Opportunities in Craft Careers***
- ***Opportunities in Electrical Trades***
- ***Opportunities in Eye Care***
- ***Opportunities in Gerontology***
- ***Opportunities in Interior Design***
- ***Opportunities in Laser Technology***

- *Opportunities in Microelectronics*
- *Opportunities in Optometry*
- *Opportunities in Pharmacy*
- *Opportunities in Public Relations*
- *Opportunities in Robotics*
- *Opportunities in Sports and Athletics*
- *Opportunities in Telecommunications*
- *Opportunities in Word Processing*

They also publish another set of books in their *"Careers in..."* series:

- *Careers in Accounting*
- *Careers in Business*
- *Careers in Communications*
- *Careers in Computers*
- *Careers in Education*
- *Careers in Engineering*
- *Careers in Health Care*
- *Careers in Science*

Also look for eight volumes in the *"Career Directory"* series published by Career Press:

- *Advertising Career Directory*
- *Book Publishing Career Directory*
- *Business and Finance Career Directory*
- *Magazine Publishing Career Directory*
- *Marketing Career Directory*
- *Newspaper Publishing Career Directory*
- *Public Relations Career Directory*
- *Travel and Hospitality Career Directory*

Walker and Company publishes a *"Career Choices"* series of books closely linked to the subject majors of college students:

- *Career Choices: Art*
- *Career Choices: Business*

Alternative Jobs and Careers 135

- *Career Choices: Communications and Journalism*
- *Career Choices: Computer Science*
- *Career Choices: Economics*
- *Career Choices: English*
- *Career Choices: History*
- *Career Choices: Law*
- *Career Choices: Mathematics*
- *Career Choices: MBA*
- *Career Choices: Political Science and Government*
- *Career Choices: Psychology*

Facts on File publishes a few books on alternative jobs and careers:

- *Career Opportunities in Art*
- *Career Opportunities in the Music Industry*
- *Career Opportunities in Television, Cable, and Video*
- *Career Opportunities in Writing*

Many other books examine a wide range of jobs and careers. Some are annual or biannual reviews of today's most popular jobs. You should find several of these books particularly helpful:

- *American Almanac of Jobs and Salaries*, John W. Wright (Avon).
- *Jobs 1991*, Ross and Kathryne Petras (Simon and Schuster).
- *101 Careers*, Michael Harkavy (Wiley).
- *Careers Encyclopedia*, Craig T. Norback ed. (National Textbook)
- *Top Professions*, Nicholas Basta (Petersons)
- *Great Careers*, Devon Cottrell Smith, ed. (Garrett Park Press).
- *The Jobs Rated Almanac*, Les Krantz (St. Martins Press).

If you are unable to find these books in your local library or bookstore, they can be ordered directly from Impact Publications. Order information is found at the end of this book. You may also want to request a copy of their free catalog of over 1,000 annotated job and career resources which includes these titles.

CONTACT ORGANIZATIONS AND PEOPLE FOR INFORMATION

While examining directories and reading books on alternative jobs and careers will provide you with useful job search information, much of this material may be too general for specifying the right job for you. In the end, the best information will come directly from people in specific jobs in specific organizations. To get this information you must interview people.

You might begin your investigations by contacting various professional and trade associations for detailed information on jobs and careers relevant to their members. For names, addresses, and telephone numbers of such associations, consult the following key directories which are available in most libraries:

- *The Encyclopedia of Associations* (Gale Research)
- *National Trade and Professional Associations* (Columbia Books)

If you are interested in jobs with a particular organization, you should contact the personnel office for information on the types of jobs offered within the organization. You may be able to examine vacancy announcements which describe the duties and responsibilities of specific jobs. If you are interested in working for federal, state, or local governments, each agency will have a personnel office which can supply you with descriptions of their jobs. While gathering such information, be sure to ask people about their jobs.

Your most productive research activity will be talking to people. Informal, word-of-mouth communication is still the most effective channel of job search information. In contrast to reading books, people have more current, detailed, and accurate information. Ask them about:

- Occupational fields
- Job requirements and training
- Interpersonal environments
- Performance expectations
- Their problems
- Salaries
- Advancement opportunities
- Future growth potential of the organization

- How best to acquire more information and contacts in a particular field

You may be surprised how willingly friends, acquaintances, and strangers will give you useful information. But before you talk to people, do your library research so that you are better able to ask thoughtful questions.

NETWORK FOR INFORMATION, ADVICE, AND REFERRALS

As you get further into your job search, networking for information, advice, and referrals will become an important element in your overall job search strategy. At that time you will come into closer contact with potential employers who can provide you with detailed information on their organizations and specific jobs. If you have a well defined MAS, specific job objectives, and a well focused resume, you should be in a good position to make networking pay off with useful information, advice, and referrals. You will quickly discover that the process of linking your MAS and objectives to specific jobs is an ongoing one involving several steps in your job search.

Chapter Twelve

USE TIME AND PLAN EFFECTIVELY

Discovering the right job requires more than just thinking about what you want to do and completing a battery of self-assessment exercises and tests in the process of conducting a job or career change. You must go far beyond trying to understand who you are and what you want to do. At the very least you must use your time wisely and develop an effective plan of action that will direct your job search into fruitful areas that lead to job interviews and offers.

WHEN IN DOUBT, TAKE ACTION

The old adage *"When in doubt, do something"* is especially relevant when expanded to include a thoughtful plan of action related to the job search process as outlined in Chapter Three: *"When in doubt, engage in a concrete activity related to the sequence of job search steps"*. This might include conducting research on communities, companies, positions, and salaries; surveying job vacancy announcements; writing a resume and job search letters; or contacting three employers each day.

But developing a plan and taking action is much easier said than done. If conducted properly, a job search can become an extremely time consuming activity. It inevitably competes with other personal and professional priorities.

That's why you need to make some initial decisions as to how and when you will conduct a job search. How much time, for example, will you set aside each day or week to engage in each of the seven job search activities outlined in Chapter Three? After you've spent numerous hours identifying your abilities and skills and formulating an objective, are you willing to commit yourself to 20 hours a week to network for information and advice? If you are unwilling to commit both your time and yourself to each activity within the process, you may remain stuck, and inevitably frustrated, at the initial stages of self-awareness and understanding. Success only comes to those who take action at other stages in the job search process.

USE TIME WISELY

If you decide to conduct your own job search with minimum assistance from professionals, your major cost will be your time. Therefore, you must find sufficient time to devote to your job search. Ask yourself this question:

> *"How valuable is my time in relation to finding a job or changing my career?"*

Assign a dollar value to your time. For example, is your time worth $3, $5, $10, $25, $50, or $100 an hour? Compare your figure with what you might pay a professional for doing much of the job search work for you. Normal professional fees range from $2,000 to $12,000.

The time you devote to your job search will depend on whether you want to work at it on a full-time or part-time basis. If you are unemployed, by all means make this a full-time endeavor -- 40 to 80 hours per week. If you are presently employed, we do not recommend quitting your job in order to look for employment. You will probably need the steady income and attendant health benefits during your transition period. Furthermore, it is easier to find new employment by appearing employed. Unemployed people project a negative image in the eyes of many employers -- they appear to need a job. **Your goal is to find a job based on your strengths rather than your needs.**

However, if you go back to school for skills retraining, your present employment status may be less relevant to employers. Your major strength is the fact that you have acquired a skill the employer needs. If you quit your job and spend money retraining, you will communicate a certain degree of risk-taking, drive, responsibility, and dedication which employers readily seek, but seldom find, in candidates today.

Assuming you will be conducting a job search on a part-time basis -- 15 to 25 hours per week -- you will need to find the necessary time for these job activities. Unfortunately, most people are busy, having programmed every hour to *"important"* personal and professional activities. Thus, conducting a job search for 15 or more hours a week means that some things will have to go or receive low priority in relation to your job search.

This is easier said than done. The job search often gets low priority. It competes with other important daily routines, such as attending meetings, taking children to games, going shopping, and watching favorite TV programs. Rather than fight with your routines -- and create family disharmony and stress -- make your job search part of your daily routines by improving your overall management of time.

Certain time management techniques will help you make your job search a high priority activity in your daily schedule. These practices may actually lower your present stress level and thus enhance your overall effectiveness.

Time management experts estimate that most people waste their time on unimportant matters. Lacking priorities, people spend 80 percent of their time on trivia and 20 percent of their time on the important matters which should get most of their attention. If you reverse this emphasis, you could have a great deal of excess time -- and probably experience less stress attendant with the common practice of crisis managing the critical 20 percent.

Before reorganizing your time, you must know how you normally use your time. Therefore, complete the following statement for a preliminary assessment of your time management behavior. While many of these statements especially pertain to individuals in managerial positions, respond to those statements that are most relevant to your employment situation.

Use Time and Plan Effectively

YOUR TIME MANAGEMENT INVENTORY

Respond to each statement by circling "yes" or "no", depending on which response best represents your normal pattern of behavior.

1. I have a written set of long, intermediate, and short-range goals for myself (and my family). — Yes / No
2. I have a clear idea of what I will do today at work and at home. — Yes / No
3. I have a clear idea of what I want to accomplish at work this coming week and month. — Yes / No
4. I set priorities and follow-through on the most important tasks first. — Yes / No
5. I judge my success by the results I produce in relation to my goals. — Yes / No
6. I use a daily, weekly, and monthly calendar for scheduling appointments and setting work targets. — Yes / No
7. I delegate as much work as possible. — Yes / No
8. I get my subordinates to organize their time in relation to mine. — Yes / No
9. I file only those things which are essential to my work. When in doubt, I throw it out. — Yes / No
10. I throw away junk mail. — Yes / No
11. My briefcase is uncluttered, including only essential materials; it serves as my office away from the office. — Yes / No

12.	I minimize the number of meetings and concentrate on making decisions rather than discussing aimlessly.	Yes	No
13.	I make frequent use of the telephone and face-to-face encounters rather than written communications.	Yes	No
14.	I make minor decisions quickly.	Yes	No
15.	I concentrate on accomplishing one thing at a time.	Yes	No
16.	I handle each piece of paper once.	Yes	No
17.	I answer most letters on the letter I receive.	Yes	No
18.	I set deadlines for myself and others and follow-through in meeting them.	Yes	No
19.	I reserve time each week to plan.	Yes	No
20.	My desk and work area are well organized and clear.	Yes	No
21.	I know how to say "no" and do so.	Yes	No
22.	I first skim books, articles, and other forms of written communication for ideas before reading further.	Yes	No
23.	I monitor my time use during the day by asking myself *"How can I best use my time at present?"*	Yes	No
24.	I deal with the present by getting things done that need to be done.	Yes	No
25.	I maintain a time log to monitor the best use of my time.	Yes	No

26.	I place a dollar value on my time and behave accordingly.	Yes	No
27.	I -- not others - control my time.	Yes	No
28.	My briefcase includes items I can work on during spare time in waiting rooms, lines, and airports.	Yes	No
29.	I keep my door shut when I'm working.	Yes	No
30.	I regularly evaluate to what degree I am achieving my stated goals.	Yes	No

If you answered *"no"* to many of these statements, you should consider incorporating a few basic time management principles and practices into your daily schedule.

Don't get to extremes by drastically restructuring your life around the *"religion"* of time management. If you followed all the advice of time management experts, you would probably alienate your family, friends, and colleagues with your narrow efficiency mentality! A realistic approach is to start monitoring your time use and then gradually re-organize your time according to goals and priorities. This is all you need to do. Forget the elaborate flow charts that are the stuff of expensive time management workshops and consultants. Start by developing a time management log that helps you monitor your present use of time. Keep daily records of how you use your time over a two week period. Identify who controls your time and the results of your time utilization. Within two weeks, clear patterns will emerge. You may learn that you have an *"open door"* policy that enables others to control your time, leaving little time to do your own work. Based on this information, you may need to close your door and be more selective about access. You may find from your analysis that most of your time is used for activities that have few if any important outcomes. If this is the case, then you may need to set goals and prioritize daily activities.

A simple yet effective technique for improving your time management practices is to complete a *"to do"* list for each day. You can purchase tablets of these forms in many stationery and office supply stores, or you can develop your own *"Things To Do Today"* list. This list also should prioritize which activities are most important to accomplish each day. Include at the top of your list a particular job search activity or several activities that should be completed on each day. If you follow this simple time management practice, you will find the necessary time to include your job search in your daily routines. You can give your job search top priority. Better still, you will accomplish more in less time, and with better results.

PLAN TO TAKE ACTION

While we recommend that you plan your job search, we also caution you to avoid the excesses of too much planning. Like time management, planning should not be all-consuming. Planning makes sense because it requires that you set goals and develop strategies for achieving the goals. However, too much planning can blind you to unexpected occurrences and opportunities. Given the highly decentralized and chaotic nature of the job market, you want to do just enough planning so you will be in a position to take advantage of what will inevitably be unexpected occurrences and opportunities arising from your planned job search activities. Therefore, as you plan your job search, be sure you are flexible enough to take advantage of new opportunities.

Based on our discussion of the sequence of job search steps in Chapter Three, we outline on page 145 a hypothetical plan for conducting an effective job search. This plan incorporates the individual job search activities over a six month period. If you phase in the first five job search steps during the initial three to four weeks and continue the final four steps in subsequent weeks and months, you should begin receiving job offers within two to three months after initiating your job search. Interviews and job offers can come anytime -- often unexpectedly -- as you conduct your job search. An average time is three months, but it can occur within a week or take as long as five months. If you plan, prepare, and persist at the job search, the pay-off will be job interviews and offers.

While three months may seem a long time, especially if you have just lost your job and you need work immediately, you can shorten your job search time by increasing the frequency of your individual job search activities. If you are job

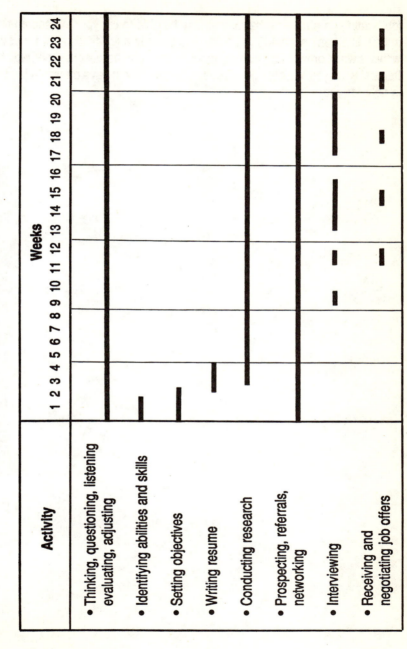

job hunting on a full-time basis, you may be able to cut your job search time in half. But don't expect to get a job -- especially a job that's right for you -- within a week or two. Job hunting requires time and hard work -- perhaps the hardest work you will ever do -- but if done properly, it pays off with a job that is right for you.

Chapter Thirteen

DEVELOP STRATEGIES FOR SUCCESS

Success is determined by more than just a good plan getting implemented. We know success is not determined primarily by intelligence, time management, or luck. Based upon experience, theory, research, common sense, and acceptance of some self-transformation principles, we believe you will achieve job search success by following many of the follwoing 20 principles:

1. **You should work hard at finding a job:** Make this a daily endeavor and involve your family.

2. **You should not be discouraged with set-backs:** You are playing the odds, so expect disappointments and handle them in stride. You will get many *"no's"* before finding the one *"yes"* which is right for you.

3. **You should be patient and persevere:** Expect three months of hard work before you connect with the job that's right for you.

4. **You should be honest with yourself and others:** Honesty is always the best policy. But don't be naive and stupid by confessing your negatives and shortcomings to others.

5. **You should develop a positive attitude toward yourself:** Nobody wants to employ guilt-ridden people with inferiority complexes. Focus on your positive characteristics.

6. **You should associate with positive and successful people:** Finding a job largely depends on how well you relate to others. Avoid associating with negative and depressing people who complain and have a *"you-can't-do-it"* attitude. Run with winners who have a positive *"can-do"* outlook on life.

7. **You should set goals:** You should have a clear idea of what you want and where you are going. Without these, you will present a confusing and indecisive image to others. Clear goals help direct your job search into productive channels. Moreover, setting high goals will help make you work hard in getting what you want.

8. **You should plan:** Convert your goals into action steps that are organized as short, intermediate, and long-range plans.

9. **You should get organized:** Translate your plans into activities, targets, names, addresses, telephone numbers, and materials. Develop an efficient and effective filing system and use a large calendar for setting time targets and recording appointments and useful information.

10. **You should be a good communicator:** Take stock of your oral, written, and nonverbal communication skills. How well do you communicate? Since most aspects of your job search involve communicating with others, and communication skills are one of the most sought-after skills, always present yourself well both verbally and nonverbally.

11. **You should be energetic and enthusiastic:** Employers are attracted to positive people. They don't like negative and depressing people who toil at their work. Generate enthusiasm both verbally and nonverbally. Check on your telephone voice - it may be more unenthusiastic than your voice in face-to-face situations.

12. **You should ask questions:** Your best information comes from asking questions. Learn to develop intelligent questions that are non-aggressive, polite, and interesting to others. But don't ask too many questions.

13. **You should be a good listener:** Being a good listener is often more important than being a good questioner and talker. Learn to improve your face-to-face listening behavior (nonverbal cues) as well as remember and use information gained from others -- if they need improving. Make others feel they enjoyed talking with you, i.e., you are one of the few people who actually *listens* to what they say.

14. **You should be polite, courteous, and thoughtful:** Treat gatekeepers, especially receptionists and secretaries, like human beings. Avoid being aggressive or too assertive. Try to be polite, courteous, and gracious. Your social graces are being observed. Remember to send thank-you letters -- a very thoughtful thing to do in a job search. Even if rejected, thank employers for the *"opportunity"* given to you. After all, they may later have additional opportunities, and they will remember you.

15. **You should be tactful:** Watch what you say to others about other people and your background. Don't be a gossip, backstabber, or confessor.

16. **You should maintain a professional stance:** Be neat in what you do and wear, and speak with the confidence, authority, and maturity of a professional.

17. **You should demonstrate your intelligence and competence:** Present yourself as someone who gets things done and achieves results -- a *producer*. Employers generally seek people who are bright, hard working, responsible, communicate well, have positive personalities, maintain good interpersonal relations, are likeable, observe dress and social codes, take initiative, are talented, possess expertise in particular areas, use good judgment, are cooperative, trustworthy, and loyal, generate confidence and credibility, and are conventional. In other words, they like people who score in the *"excellent"* to *"outstanding"* categories of the annual performance evaluation.

18. **You should not overdo your job search:** Don't engage in overkill and bore everyone with your *"job search"* stories. Achieve balance in everything you do. Occasionally take a few days off to do nothing related to your job search. Develop a system of incentives and rewards -- such as two non-job search days a week, if you accomplish targets A, B, C, and D.

19. **You should be open-minded and keep an eye open for *"luck":*** Too much planning can blind you to unexpected and fruitful opportunities. You should welcome serendipity. Learn to re-evaluate your goals and strategies. Seize new opportunities if they appear appropriate.

20. **You should evaluate your progress and adjust:** Take two hours once every two weeks and evaluate what you are doing and accomplishing. If necessary, tinker with your plans and reorganize your activities and priorities. Don't become too routinized and thereby kill creativity and innovation.

These principles should provide you with an initial orientation for starting your job search. As you become more experienced, you will develop your own set of operating principles that should work for you in particular employment situations.

Chapter Fourteen

DISCOVER THE RIGHT RESOURCES

Success in finding the right job also involves knowing which resources are the most useful for conducting a job search. While you chose this book as one of your resources, you should also discover many other resources that complement as well as extend this book into other critical job search steps.

Throughout this book we have mentioned several resources we feel will assist you at various stages in assessing your motivated abilities and skills, formulating a job objective, and identifying jobs appropriate for your particular mix of interests, values, abilities, skills, and objectives. Let's now turn to what we consider to be some of the best resources available for further expanding your job search beyond this book as we attempt to bring some coherence and organization to this literature to assist you in identifying any additional resources that might be useful to you in your job search. Since many of these books cannot be found in local bookstores or libraries, you may need to order them directly from the publishers. For your convenience, you can order most of the books through IMPACT PUBLICATIONS by completing the order form at the end of this book. For a more complete listing of career planning and job search resources, contact our publisher to receive a free copy of their annotated catalog of over 1,000 resources.

We only deal with books here, because they are the least expensive and most easily accessible resources in bookstores and libraries. However, more and more computer software programs are now available to assist you with two stages in your job search: self-assessment and resume writing. As mentioned in previous chapters, many career planning centers and some libraries and computer stores offer these resources.

CHOOSING WHAT'S BEST FOR YOU

During the past 20 years hundreds of self-help books have been written on how to find a job and advance one's career. Each year dozens of additional volumes are published to inform as well as enlighten a growing audience of individuals concerned with conducting a proper job search.

You may be initially overwhelmed with the sheer volume of the career planning and job search literature available to help individuals find jobs and change careers. Once you examine a few books you will quickly learn that this literature is designed to be *used*. The books are not designed to describe or explain reality, develop a theory, nor predict the future.

Most career planning and job search books are designed to **advance self-help strategies** based upon the particular ideas or experiences of individual writers. They expound a **set of beliefs** -- more or less logical and based on both experience and faith. Like other how-to literature on achieving success, you must first **believe** in these books before you can make them work for you. These books must be judged on the basis of faith and usefulness.

Given the nature of this literature, your best approach is to **pick and choose** which books are **more or less useful** for you. There is nothing magical about these books. At best, they may challenge your preconceptions; develop alternative beliefs which you may or may not find acceptable; provide you with some directions; and help motivate you to implement an effective job search. They will not get you a job.

The level of redundancy in this literature may disturb many readers. Moreso than in many other fields, career planning writers tend to quote each other or rely on the perspectives of a few key writers in restating the same approaches in a different form. As a result, many individuals confuse the high level of redundancy as repeated evidence of career and job *"facts"*.

WHAT YOU GET

We have examined most of the career planning and job search literature with a view toward identifying the best of the lot. We've judged the literature in terms of its degree of accuracy, realism, comprehensiveness, and usefulness. In doing so, we have found three major types of books which use different approaches to getting a job:

- Books designed to teach individuals key job search **process and strategy skills**; these books emphasize *"how"* questions.

- Books designed to outline various **employment fields**; these books emphasize *"what"* and *"where"* questions.

- Books designed to address key career issues for **special groups**; these books emphasize *"what"* and *"how"* questions.

A growing number of comprehensive job search books attempt to apply the process and strategy skills to different employment fields and special groups.

Process and Strategy Skills

The first type of career planning and job search literature concentrates primarily on developing **process and strategy skills**. Most of these books tell you *how* to develop an effective job search regardless of your particular employment field or your specialized needs. They seldom address substantive **what** and **where** questions central to finding any job. You are left to answer these questions on your own or by using other resources which focus on what jobs are available and where you can find them.

There are no surprises in this literature since most of the books follow a similar pattern in approaching the subject. The major difference is that the books are more or less readable. Most of these process books are preoccupied with *"getting in touch with yourself"* by emphasizing the need to *"know what you want to do today, tomorrow, and the rest of your life"*. Some of this literature is rightly referred to as *"touchy-feely"* because of its concern with trying to get to know yourself -- the basis for self-assessment. A mainstay of psychologists, counselors, and activity-oriented trainers, this type of positive, up-beat literature is at best designed to reorient your life around (1) identifying what is right about yourself (your strengths), and (2) setting goals based upon an understanding of your past and present in the hope you will do better in the future (your objectives).

The real strengths of this literature lie in orienting your thinking along new lines, providing you with some baseline information on your strengths and goals, and providing you with positive motivation for developing and implementing an effective job search strategy. If you're looking for specifics, such as learning what the jobs are and where you can find them, this literature will disappoint you with its vagueness.

Placed within our career planning framework in Chapter Three, much of this process and strategy literature falls into the initial two steps of our career planning process: self-assessment and objective setting. Examples of career planning literature using this approach are the popular books written by Bolles, Miller and Mattson, Crystal, and Sher: *Where Do I Go From Here With My Life?*, *What Color Is Your Parachute?*, *The Three Boxes of Life*, *The Truth About You*, and *Wishcraft*. Other books, such as Dahl and Sykes' *Charting Your Goals*, the Gales' *Discover What You're Best At*, Yeager's *CareerMap*, Chapman's *Be True to Your Future*, and Pilkington's *The Real-Life Aptitude Test*, provide useful exercises for identifying goals and assessing abilities and skills. You should read these books if you lack a clear understanding of who you are, what you want to do, and where you are going. They will help you get in touch with yourself before you get in touch with employers!

Several books focus on additional steps in the career planning and job search processes, such as doing research, writing resumes and letters, networking, interviewing, and negotiating salaries. While also emphasizing process and strategy, these are more comprehensive books than the others. Some books include all of the job search steps whereas others concentrate on one or two. Examples of the most comprehensive such books include those written by Krannich, Wegmann and Chapman, Hecklinger and Curtin, Lathrop, Jackson, Figler, Irish, Snelling, and Studner: *Careering and Re-Careering for the 1990s, The Right Place at the Right Time, Training For Life, Who's Hiring Who, The Complete Job Search Handbook, Guerrilla Tactics in the Job Market, Go Hire Yourself an Employer, The Right Job*, and *Super Job Search*.

You will find hundreds of books that focus on the *research stage* of the job search. Most of these books are geographic, field, or organizational directories or job banks which list names and addresses of potential employers. Examples include the Bob Adams' *Job Bank Series* on 18 major cities and metropolitan areas, Surrey Book's *How to Get a Job In...* series on nine cities, Random House's *How to Be Happily Employed In...*, Wright's *The American Almanac of Jobs and Salaries,* Petras' *Jobs 1991,* Krantz's *The Jobs Rated Almanac,* Snelling's *Jobs!,* Schwartz's and Brechner's *The Career Finder,* Plunkett's *The Almanac of American Employers,* Levering's *100 Best Companies to Work for in America,* Levine's *Corporate Address Book,* and Dun and Bradstreet's *The Career Guide: Dun's Employment Opportunity Directory.* Job search approaches relating to much of this literature are in sharp contrast to approaches of the standard career planning literature. Directories, for example, should be used to gather information -- names, addresses, and phone numbers -- to be used in targeting one's networking activities rather than as sources for shotgunning resumes and letters.

Numerous books are written on other key job search steps -- especially resume and letter writing and job interviews. The ***resume and letter writing*** books fall into two major categories:

- Books designed to walk you through the process of developing a resume based upon a thorough understanding of each step in the job search process. Examples include Krannich's and Banis' *High Impact Resumes and Letters,* Jackson's *The Perfect Resume,* Fry's *Your First Resume,* Swanson's *The Resume Solution,* and Good's *Does Your Resume Wear Blue Jeans?, Does Your Resumes Wear Apron Strings?,* and *Does Your Resume Wear Combat Boots?*

- Books primarily presenting examples of resumes and letters. Examples of such books are numerous -- most resume and letter writing books you will find in libraries and bookstores fall in this category. One of the best such books is Parker's *The Resume Catalog.* Others include Frank's *200 Letters for Job Hunters,* Hansen's *Dynamic Cover Letters,* Beatty's *The Perfect Cover Letter,* and the Krannichs' *Dynamite Resumes* and *Dynamite Cover Letters.*

The first type of resume and letter writing book urges the user to develop resumes and letters that represent the *"unique you"* in relation to specific positions and employers. Incorporating much of the approach used in this book, they emphasize the importance of finding a job that is right for you rather than try to adjust your experience to fit into a job that may be inappropriate for you. These books are based upon a particular approach to finding a job as outlined in several of the comprehensive career planning and job search books.

The second type of resume and letter writing book lacks a clear approach other than an implied suggestion that readers should creatively plagiarize the examples. In other words, good resumes and letters are produced by osmosis! A few resume books, such as those mentioned above as well as Schuman's and Lewis' **Revising Your Resume** and Yate's **Resumes That Knock 'Em Dead**, fall between these two types.

Several books address *networking*. Most of these books, however, focus on formal networks relevant to women rather than on the process of networking for everyone. Examples include Kleiman's **Women's Networks** and Stern's **Is Networking For You?** While several job search books include a short section on networking -- discuss the importance of networking and give a few examples of networks and networking -- the Krannichs' **Network Your Way to Career and Job Success** is the only book to focus solely on the role of networking in the job search process. Boe and Young's **Is Your "Net" Working** looks at how to build contacts for career development. Other books such as Baber and Waymon's **Great Connections** and Roane's **How to Work a Room**, approach networking from the perspective of small talk in particular social settings.

You will also find several *job interview* books designed for both interviewees and interviewers. Most of these books examine each step in the interview process -- from preparation to negotiating salary. Some of these books, such as Yate's **Knock 'Em Dead** and Allen's **The Complete Q & A Job Interview Book**, focus primarily on questions and answers. Other books, such as the Krannichs' **Interview for Success**, are more comprehensive, including interview settings, types of interviews, and nonverbal communication along with a discussion of appropriate questions and answers. Some of the better interview books are written by Vik, Meyer and Berchtold, and Medley: **Interviews That Get Results, Getting the Job,** and **Sweaty Palms.**

While most comprehensive job search and interview books include a section on salary negotiations, a few books have been written on this subject. However, some of these books are now out of print, but they may be available in your local library. Examples include the Krannichs' *Salary Success*, Kennedy's *Salary Strategies*, Chastain's *Winning the Salary Game*, and Chapman's *How to Make $1000 a Minute*. Much of the general literature on negotiation tactics is relevant to this topic.

Specific Employment Fields

A second type of career and job search literature focuses primarily on specific employment fields. These books come in many forms. Some are designed to give the reader a general overview of what type of work is involved in each field. Other books include educational training and job search strategies appropriate for entry into each field. And still others are annotated listings of job and career titles -- the most comprehensive being the Department of Labor's *Occupational Outlook Handbook* and *The Dictionary of Occupational Titles*.

The majority of books on employment fields are designed for individuals who are considering a particular employment field rather than for individuals wishing to advance within a field. As such, most of these books are general introductions designed to answer important "what", "where", and "how" questions for high school and college students. They provide little useful information for older and more experienced professionals. Examples of such books include the 138 volumes in National Textbook's *Opportunities In... Series* with such titles as *Opportunities In Architecture, Opportunities In Office Occupations, Opportunities In Public Relations, Opportunities In Forestry,* and *Opportunities In Travel Careers*. More and more books are being produced in specific employment fields, especially for computer, business, medical, government, international, communication, media, and travel specialists. In Chapter Eleven we identified several of these books.

Specialized Career Groups

A final set of career planning and job search books has emerged during the past few years. These books are designed for specific groups of job seekers who supposedly need specialized assistance not found in most general job search process and employment field books. The most common such books focus on women, minorities, the handicapped, immigrants, public employees, military personnel, educators, mobile spouses, college graduates, children, and teenagers.

Many of these books represent a new type of career planning book that has emerged during the past few years and will most likely continue in the foreseeable future. Several books deal with both *process* and *substance*. They link the substantive *"what"* and *"where"* concerns of specific employment fields to *"how"* processes appropriately outlined for each field.

Take, for example, the field of advertising. Several books, such as Caffrey's **So You Want to Be in Advertising**, Mogal's **Making It in the Media Professions**, and Fry's **The Advertising Career Directory**, now outline the jobs available in the field of advertising (*what questions*), where you should look for vacancies (*where questions*), and the best strategies for finding a job, including resumes, letters, and interview questions appropriate for the advertising field (*how questions*).

These specialized career books finally identify how general job search strategies must be adapted and modified to respond to the employment needs of different types of individuals as well as to the employment cultures found in different fields. Some of the most popular such books include **The Black Woman's Career Guide, Job Hunting For the Disabled, Getting a Job in the United States, The Complete Guide to Public Employment, The Complete Guide to International Jobs and Careers, The Educator's Guide to Alternative Jobs and Careers, Alternative Careers for Teachers, The Relocating Spouse's Guide to Employment, Retiring From the Military, Liberal Arts Jobs,** and **Summer Opportunities For Kids and Teenagers**.

In the coming decade we can expect to see more career planning books produced along these combined process, field, and group lines. While general career planning books focusing only on process and strategy will continue to proliferate, the real excitement in this field will be centered around the continuing development of resources which link process to specific employment fields and specialized groups. If, for example, you are in the fields of real estate or robotics, you should be able to find books outlining what the jobs are, where to find them, and how to get them. Such books will most likely be written by seasoned professionals in particular fields and representing specialized groups rather than by career planning professionals who are primarily trained in process skills. Such books will meet a growing need for information from individuals who have a solid understanding of how to get a job based on familiarity with the *"ins"* and *"outs"* of each field.

The following bibliography includes some of the best career planning books available today. Consistent with the structure of this book and our discussion of career planning and job search literature, we have organized the bibliography according to process, field, and group categories.

BIBLIOGRAPHY

Job Search Strategies and Tactics

Figler, Howard E., ***The Complete Job Search Handbook*** (New York: Holt, Rinehart, and Winston, 1988).

Hecklinger, Fred J. and Bernadette M. Curtin, ***Training For Life: A Practical Guide To Career and Life Planning*** (Dubuque, IA: Kendell/Hunt Publishing, 1988).

Irish, Richard K., ***Go Hire Yourself An Employer*** (New York: Doubleday, 1987).

Jackson, Tom, ***Guerrilla Tactics In the Job Market*** (New York: Bantam, 1980).

Kennedy, Joyce Lain and Darryl Laramore, ***The Joyce Lain Kennedy's Career Book*** (Lincolnwood, IL: National Textbook, 1988).

Krannich, Ronald L., ***Careering and Re-Careering For the 1990s*** (Woodbridge, VA: Impact Publications, 1991).

Lathrop, Richard, ***Who's Hiring Who*** (Berkeley, CA: Ten Speed Press, 1989).

Rogers, Edward J., ***Getting Hired*** (Englewood, NJ: Prentice Hall, 1982).

Sher, Barbara, ***Wishcraft: How To Get What You Really Want*** (New York: Ballantine, 1983).

Snelling, Sr., Robert O., *The Right Job* (New York: Viking Penguin, 1987).

Stanat, Kirby W., *Job Hunting Secrets & Tactics* (Piscataway, NJ: New Century Publishers, 1977).

Studner, Peter K., *Super Job Search* (Los Angeles, CA: Jamenair Ltd., 1987).

Wegmann, Robert and Robert Chapman, *The Right Place at the Right Time* (Berkeley, CA: Ten Speed Press, 1990).

Wegmann, Robert, Robert Chapman, and Miriam Johnson, *Work in the New Economy* (Indianapolis, IN: JIST Works, 1989).

Skills Identification, Testing, and Self-Assessment

Bolles, Richard N., *The New Quick Job Hunting Map* (Berkeley, CA: Ten Speed Press, 1990).

Bolles, Richard N., *The Three Boxes of Life* (Berkeley, CA: Ten Speed Press, 1981).

Bolles, Richard N., *What Color Is Your Parachute?* (Berkeley, CA: Ten Speed Press, 1991).

Branden, Nathaniel, *How To Raise Your Self-Esteem* (New York: Bantam, 1986).

Crystal, John C. and Richard N. Bolles, *Where Do I Go From Here With My Life?* (Berkeley, CA: Ten Speed Press, 1979).

Dahl, Dan and Randolph Sykes, *Charting Your Goals* (New York: Harper and Row, 1988).

Gale, Barry and Linda Gale, *Discover What You're Best At* (New York: Simon & Schuster, 1990).

Holland, John L., **Making Vocational Choices** (Englewood Cliffs, NJ: Prentice-Hall, 1985).

Miller, Arthur F. and Ralph T. Mattson, **The Truth About You: Discover What You Should Be Doing With Your Life** (Berkeley, CA: Ten Speed Press, 1989).

Krannich, Ronald L. and Caryl Rae, **Discover the Right Job for You!** (Woodbridge, VA: Impact Publications, 1991).

Pilkington, Maya, **The Real-Life Aptitude Test** (New York: St. Martin's Press, 1989).

Sheele, Adele, **Skills for Success** (New York: Ballantine, 1979).

Research on Cities, Fields, and Organizations

Adams Inc., Bob (ed.), **The Job Bank Series: Atlanta, Boston, Chicago, Dallas, Denver, Detroit, Florida, Houston, Los Angeles, Minneapolis, New York, Ohio, Philadelphia, San Francisco, Seattle, St. Louis, Washington, DC** (Boston, MA: Bob Adams, Inc., 1989-1991).

Adams Inc., Bob (ed.), **The National Job Bank** (Boston, MA: Bob Adams, Inc., 1990).

Basta, Nicholas, **Top Professions** (Princeton, NJ: Peterson's Guides, 1989).

Berreto, Helena, **California: Where to Work, Where to Live** (Rocklin, CA: Prima Publishing and Communications, 1989.

Camden, Bishop, Schwartz, Greene, Fleming-Holland, **"How To Get a Job in..." Insider's City Guides: Atlanta, Chicago, Houston, Dallas/Ft. Worth, Los Angeles/San Diego, New York, San Francisco, Seattle/Portland, Washington, DC** (Chicago, IL: Surrey, 1989-1990).

Career Associates, *Career Choices: Art, Business, Communications and Journalism, Computer Science, Economics, English, History, Law, Mathematics, MBA, Political Science and Government, Psychology* (New York: Walker and Co., 1990).

Career Press, *The Career Directory Series: Advertising, Book Publishing, Business and Finance, Magazine Publishing, Marketing, Newspaper Publishing, Public Relations, Travel and Hospitality* (Hawthorne, NJ: The Career Press, 1990).

Harkavy, Michael, *101 Careers* (New York, Wiley, 1990).

Harrington, Thomas F. and Arthur J. O'Shea (eds.), *Guide for Occupational Exploration* (Circle Pines, MN: American Guidance Service, 1989).

Hopke, William (ed.), *Encyclopedia of Careers and Vocational Guidance* (Chicago, IL: J. G. Ferguson, 1990).

Krantz, Less, *The Jobs Rated Almanac* (New York: Pharos Books, 1988).

Levering, Robert, Milton Moskowitz, and Michael Katz, *The 100 Best Companies To Work For In America* (Chicago, IL: NAL, 1985).

Norback, Craig T., *Careers Encyclopedia* (Lincolnwood, IL: National Textbook, 1988).

Petras, Ross and Kathryn, *Jobs 1991* (New York: Simon & Schuster, 1991).

Plunkett, Jack W., *The Almanac of American Employers* (Chicago, IL: Contemporary Books, 1985).

Schwartz, Lester and Irv Brechner, *The Career Finder* (New York: Ballantine, 1990).

U.S. Department of Labor, *Dictionary of Occupational Titles* (Washington, DC: U.S. Department of Labor, 1977).

U.S. Department of Labor, *The Occupational Outlook Handbook* (Washington, DC: U.S. Department of Labor, 1990).

Wright, John W., *The American Almanac of Jobs and Salaries* (New York: Avon, 1990).

Resumes and Letters

Beatty, Richard H., *The Perfect Cover Letter* (New York: Wiley, 1989).

Bostwick, Burdette E., *Resume Writing* (New York: Wiley, 1984).

Fitzpatrick, William G. and C. Edward Good, *Does Your Resume Wear Combat Boots?* (Charlottesville, VA: Blue Jeans Press, 1990).

Frank, William S., *200 Letters for Job Hunters* (Berkeley, CA: Ten Speed Press, 1990).

Fry, Ronald W., *Your First Resume* (Hawthorne, NJ: Career Press, 1989).

Good, C. Edward, *Does Your Resume Wear Apron Strings?* (Charlottesville, VA: Blue Jeans Press, 1989).

Good, C. Edward, *Does Your Resume Wear Blue Jeans?* (Charlottesville, VA: Blue Jeans Press, 1985).

Hansen, Katherine, *Dynamic Cover Letters* (Berkeley, CA: Ten Speed Press, 1990).

Jackson, Tom, *The Perfect Resume* (New York: Doubleday, 1990).

Kaplan, Robbie Miller, *Sure-Hire Resumes* (New York: AMACOM, 1990).

Krannich, Ronald L. and Caryl Rae, *Dynamite Cover Letters* (Woodbridge, VA: Impact Publications: 1991).

Krannich, Ronald L. and Caryl Rae, **Dynamite Resumes** (Woodbridge, VA: Impact Publications, 1991).

Krannich, Ronald L. and William Banis, **High Impact Resumes and Letters** (Woodbridge, VA: Impact Publications, 1990).

Parker, Yana, **The Damn Good Resume Guide** (Berkeley, NY: Ten Speed Press, 1986).

Parker, Yana, **The Resume Catalog** (Berkeley, NY: Ten Speed Press, 1988).

Schuman, Nancy and William Lewis, **Revising Your Resume** (New York: Wiley, 1987).

Yate, Martin John, **Resumes That Knock 'Em Dead** (Holbrook, MA: Bob Adams, 1988).

Networking

Baber, Ann and Lynne Waymon, **Great Connections: Small Talk and Networking for Businesspeople** (Woodbridge, VA: Impact Publications, 1991).

Boe, Anne and Bettie B. Youngs, **Is Your "Net" Working?** (New York: Wiley, 1989).

Kleiman, Carol, **Women's Networks** (New York: Ballantine, 1982).

Krannich, Ronald L. and Caryl Rae Krannich, **Network Your Way To Job and Career Success** (Manassas, VA: Impact Publications, 1989).

Raye-Johnson, Venda, **Effective Networking** (Palo Alto, CA: Crisp Publications, 1990).

Roane, Susan, **How to Work a Room** (New York: Warner Books, 1989).

Dress, Appearance, and Image

Bixler, Susan, *The Professional Image* (New York: Putnam, 1984).

Jackson, Carole, *Color Me Beautiful* (Washington, DC: Acropolis, 1986).

Karpinski, Kenneth J., *The Winner's Style* (Washington, DC: Acropolis Press, 1987).

Martin, Judith, *Miss Manners' Guide to the Turn-of-the-Millennium* (New York: St. Martin's Press, 1989).

Molloy, John T., *Dress For Success* (New York: Warner, 1988).

Molloy, John T., *The Woman's Dress For Success Book* (New York: Warner, 1977).

Nicholson, JoAnne and Judy Lewis-Crum, *Color Wonderful* (New York: Bantam, 1986).

Stran, Pamela Redmond, *Dressing Smart* (New York: Doubleday, 1990).

Wallach, Janet, *Working Wardrobe* (New York: Warner, 1981).

Interviews and Salary Negotiations

Beatty, R. H., *The Five Minute Interview* (New York: Wiley, 1986).

Chapman, Jack, *How To Make $1000 A Minute: Negotiating Salaries and Raises* (Berkeley, CA: Ten Speed Press, 1987).

Chastain, Sherry, *Winning the Salary Game* (New York: Wiley, 1990).

Kennedy, Marilyn Moats, *Salary Strategies* (New York: Scribners, 1982).

Krannich, Caryl Rae and Ronald L. Krannich, *Interview For Success* (Woodbridge, VA: Impact Publications, 1990).

Krannich, Ronald L. and Caryl Rae Krannich, *Salary Success* (Woodbridge, VA: Impact Publications, 1990).

Medley, H. Anthony, *Sweaty Palms* (Berkeley, CA: Ten Speed Press, 1984).

Meyer, Mary Coeli and Inge M. Berchtold, *Getting the Job: How to Interview Successfully* (Princeton, NJ: Petrocelli, 1982).

Vlk, Suzee, *Interviews That Get Results* (New York: Simon & Schuster, 1984).

Yate, Martin John, *Knock 'Em Dead With Great Answers to Tough Interview Questions* (Holbrook, MA: Bob Adams, Inc., 1990).

Educators

Bastress, Fran, *Teachers In New Careers* (Cranston, RI: Carroll Press, 1984).

Krannich, Ronald L., *The Educator's Guide to Alternative Jobs and Careers* (Woodbridge, VA: Impact Publications, 1991).

Pollack, Sandy, *Alternative Careers For Teachers* (Boston, MA: Harvard Common Press, 1986).

Public-Oriented Careers

Krannich, Ronald L. and Caryl Rae Krannich, *The Almanac of American Government Jobs and Careers* (Woodbridge, VA: Impact Publications, 1990).

Krannich, Ronald L. and Caryl Rae Krannich, *The Complete Guide to Public Employment* (Woodbridge, VA: Impact Publications, 1990).

Krannich, Ronald L. and Caryl Rae Krannich, *Find a Federal Job Fast!* (Woodbridge, VA: Impact Publications, 1990).

Lauber, Daniel, *The Compleat Guide To Finding Jobs In Government* (Evanston, IL: Planning/Communications, 1989).

McAdams, Terry W., *Careers In the Nonprofit Sector* (Washington, DC: The Taft Group, 1986).

Smith, Devon Cottrell (ed.), *Great Careers: The Fourth of July Guide to Careers, Internships, and Volunteer Opportunities in the Nonprofit Sector* (Garrett Park, MD: Garrett Park Press, 1990).

Waelde, David E., *How To Get a Federal Job* (Washington, DC: FEDHELP, 1989).

Wood, Patricia B., *The 171 Reference Book* (Washington, DC: Workbooks, Inc., 1986).

International and Overseas Jobs

Beckmann, David M., Timothy J. Mitchell, and Linda L. Powers, *The Overseas List* (Minneapolis, MN: Augsburg Publishing, 1986).

Casewit, Curtis W., *How To Get a Job Overseas* (New York: Prentice-Hall, 1984).

Foreign Policy Association (ed.), *Guide To Careers In World Affairs* (New York: Foreign Policy Association, 1987).

Kocher, Eric, *International Jobs* (Reading, MA: Addison-Wesley, 1989).

Krannich, Ronald L. and Caryl Rae Krannich, *The Almanac of International Jobs and Careers* (Woodbridge, VA: Impact Publications, 1990).

Krannich, Ronald L. and Caryl Rae Krannich, *The Complete Guide to International Jobs and Careers* (Woodbridge, VA: Impact Publications, 1990).

Win, David, *International Careers: An Insider's Guide* (Charlotte, VT: Williamson Publishing, 1987).

Military

Bradley, Jeff, *A Young Person's Guide To the Military* (Boston, MA: Harvard Common Press, 1987).

Garlock, Michael, *From Soldier To Civilian* (New York: Prentice-Hall, 1988).

Marrs, Texe and Karen Read, *The Woman's Guide to Military Service* (Cockeysville, MD: Liberty Publishing, 1986).

Nyman, Keith O., *Re-Entry: Turning Military Experience Into Civilian Success* (Harrisonburg, PA: Stackpole Books, 1990).

Women and Spouses

Bastress, Fran, *The Relocating Spouse's Guide To Employment* (Chevy Chase, MD: Woodley Publications, 1989).

Catalyst, *What to Do With the Rest of Your Life* (New York: Simon & Schuster, 1980).

Lewis, William and Nancy Schuman, *Back to Work: A Career Guide for the Returnee* (Woodbury, NY: Barron's, 1985).

Nivens, Beatryce, *Careers for Women Without College Degrees* (New York: McGraw-Hill, 1988).

Zeitz, Daila and Lorraine Dusky, *The Best Companies For Women* (New York: Simon & Schuster, 1988).

College Students

Career Associates, *"Career Choices in..." Series: Art, Business, Communications and Journalism, Computer Science, Economics, English, History, Law, Mathematics, MBA, Political Science and Government,* and *Psychology.*

Falvey, Jack, *After College: The Business of Getting Jobs* (Charlotte, VT: Williamson Publishing, 1986).

Fox, Marcia R., *Put Your Degree to Work* (New York: W. W. Norton, 1988).

LaFevre, John L., *How You Really Get Hired* (New York: Simon & Schuster, 1989).

Lento-McGovern, Diane, *Life After College: Which Direction Is Best for You?* (White Hall, VA: Betterway Publications, 1986).

Munschauer, John L., *Jobs for English Majors and Other Smart People* (Princeton, NJ: Peterson's Guides, 1986).

Nadler, Burton Jay, *Liberal Arts Jobs* (Princeton, NJ: Peterson's Guides, 1985).

Phifer, Paul, *College Majors and Careers* (Garrett Park, MD: Garrett Park Press, 1987).

Reyes-Guerra, David R. and Allan M. Fischer, *The Engineering/High Tech Student's Handbook* (Princeton, NJ: Peterson's Guides, 1990).

Children, Youth, and Summer Jobs

Billy, Christopher (ed.), *Summer Opportunities For Kids and Teenagers* (Princeton, NJ: Peterson's Guides, 1990).

Bouchard, Jerry, *Graduating to the 9-5 World* (Woodbridge, VA: Impact Publications, 1991).

Catalyst, *It's Your Future: Catalyst's Career Guide For High School Girls* (Princeton, NJ: Peterson's Guides, 1982).

Children's Dictionary of Occupations (Bloomington, IL: Meridian Educational Corp., 1985).

Douglas, Martha, *Go For It!* (Berkeley, CA: Ten Speed Press, 1983).

Greenberg, Jan W., *The Teenager's Guide to the Best Summer Opportunities* (Boston, MA: Harvard Common Press, 1985).

Lee, Rose P., *A Real Job For You: An Employment Guide For Teens* (White Hall, VA: Betterway Publications, 1984).

Minorities, Immigrants, and Disabled

Friedenberg, Joan E. and Curtis H. Bradley, *Finding a Job In the United States* (Lincolnwood, IL: National Textbook, 1986).

Hoffa, Helynn and Gary Morgan, *Yes You Can* (New York, St. Martin's, 1990).

Johnson, Willis L. (ed.), *Directory of Special Programs For Minority Group Members* (Garrett Park, MD: Garrett Park Press, 1991).

Lewis, Adele and Edith Marks, *Job Hunting For the Disabled* (Woodbury, NY: Barron's, 1983).

Nivens, Beatryce, *The Black Woman's Career Guide* (New York: Doubleday, 1987).

Experienced and Elderly

Birsner, E. Patricia, *The 40+ Job Hunting Guide* (New York: Facts on File, 1990).

Falvey, Jack, *What's Next? Career Strategies After 35* (Charlotte, VT: Williamson Publishing, 1986).

Morgan, John S., *Getting a Job After 50* (Blue Ridge Summit, PA: TAB Books, 1987).

Myers, Albert and Christopher Anderson, *Success Over Sixty* (New York: Simon & Schuster, 1986).

Alternative Career Fields

Boyd, Wilma, *Travel Agent* (New York: Arco, 1989).

Edward, Kenneth W., *Your Successful Real Estate Career* (New York: AMACOM, 1987).

Field, Shelly, *Career Opportunities in the Music Industry* (New York: Facts on File, 1986).

Hawes, Gene R. and Douglas L. Brownstone, *The Outdoor Careers Guide* (New York: Facts on File, 1986).

Mogel, Leonard, *Making It in the Media Professions* (Chester, CT: The Globe Pequot Press, 1988).

New Accountant Co., *New Accountant Careers* (Glen Cove, NY: New Accountant Co., 1989).

"Opportunities In..." Career Series (138 titles), (Lincolnwood, IL: National Textbook, 1984-1991).

Peterson's, *Job Opportunities for Business and Liberal Arts Graduates* (Princeton, NJ: Peterson's Guides, 1991).

Peterson's, *Job Opportunities for Engineering, Science, and Computer Graduates* (Princeton, NJ: Peterson's Guides, 1991).

Rubin, K., *Flying High In Travel: A Complete Guide To Careers In the Travel Industry* (New York: Wiley, 1986).

Rucker, T. Donald and Martin D. Keller, *Planning Your Medical Career* (Garrett Park, MD: Garrett Park Press, 1987).

INDEX

A
Abilities, 35, 38-48
Accomplishments, 47, 64
Achievements, 64, 67-72
Action, 19
Analysis, 65
Apprenticeships, 88
Approaches, 4-6, 30-37
Armed Forces training, 88-89
Assessment centers, 27
Assumptions, 32-33
Autobiography of accomplishments, 7, 66-67

B
Behavior, 31, 79
Bolles, 31, 46, 65
Breakthrough thinking, 78-79

C
Career:
    changes, 41
    conferences, 28
Career development process, 15-19
Careering competencies, 9-12
Careers, 14
Change, 78-79

Checklist method, 46
Colleges, 24-25, 90
Community colleges, 24-25, 89
Computer programs:
    interests and values, 62-63
    job matching, 131
    skills assessment, 47-48

D
Discipline, 80

E
Education, 82-95
Employers, 97-98
Entrepreneurs, 83
Executive search firms, 25-26

F
Future, 63, 99-117

G
Goals, 80, 96-121

H
Haldane Associates, 65
Headhunters, 25-26

Historical determinism, 77
Holland, 53, 55, 74
Home study, 89

I

Interests, 35, 49-63
Interpersonal environments, 61-62
Interviews, 156

J

Job:
    alternatives, 35, 122-137
    banks, 15
    fairs, 28
    finding, 13-20
    fit, 3
    frustrations, 59
    information, 19
    loss, 42
    market, 14
    research, 132-135
    satisfaction, 2
    search, 2, 17-20
    services, 21-29

M

Marketing services, 26
Miller and Mattson, 74, 123
Motivated skills and abilities (MAS), 32, 35-36, 64-75
Motivated Skills Exercise, 67-73
Motivations, 35, 77
Myers-Briggs Type Indicator, 27, 54

N

Networking, 36, 137

O

Objectives:
    future, 63
    general, 36
    job, 36, 96-121
    role of, 3

P

Patterns, 36, 64-75, 78
People Management, Inc., 65
Placement offices, 24-25
Planning, 80, 144-146
Positive thinking, 5-6
Private employment agencies, 24
Professional associations, 28
Professionals, 21-29
Public employment services, 23-24

Q

Qualifications, 42, 46

R

Realism, 79-82, 98-99
Redundancy, 74-75
Resources, 4, 7, 91-94, 151-171
Resumes, 155-156
Risk takers, 83

S

Self-assessment, 18, 30, 36
Self-directed approaches, 31, 34
Self-transformation, 5-6, 32, 34, 76-95
SIMA, 123
Skills:
    job search, 18
    functional, 43-46
    Map, 46-47, 65-66
    transferable, 43-46
    work-content, 15, 35, 39
Strength identification, 72
Strengths, 19, 35, 40-42
Strong-Campbell Interest Inventory, 27, 54
Success:
    strategies, 147-150
    thinking, 80

T

Testing:
    centers, 27
    instruments, 54

Thinking, 78-79
Time management, 138-144
Training, 83-95

U
Universities, 24-25, 90

V
Vacancy announcements, 2
Values, 35, 49-63
Vocational education, 86

W
Weaknesses, 42
Women's centers, 27
Work:
    interests, 49-55
    values, 55-62

CAREER RESOURCES

Call or write IMPACT PUBLICATIONS to receive a free copy of their latest comprehensive, illustrated, and annotated catalog of over 1,000 career resources.

The following career resources are available directly from Impact Publications. Complete the following form or list the titles, include postage (see formula at the end), enclose payment, and send your order to:

> **IMPACT PUBLICATIONS**
> 4580 Sunshine Court
> Woodbridge, VA 22192
> Tel. 703/361-7300
> FAX 703/335-9486

Orders from individuals must be prepaid by check, moneyorder, Visa or MasterCard number. We accept telephone and FAX orders with a Visa or MasterCard number.

Qty.	TITLES	Price	TOTAL

JOB SEARCH STRATEGIES AND TACTICS

Qty.	Title	Price	Total
___	Careering and Re-Careering for the 1990s	$12.95	___
___	Complete Job Search Handbook	$12.95	___
___	Go Hire Yourself an Employer	$9.95	___
___	Joyce Lane Kennedy's Career Book	$29.95	___
___	The Right Place at the Right Time	$11.95	___
___	Super Job Search	$24.95	___
___	Wishcraft	$7.95	___
___	Who's Hiring Who	$10.95	___

SKILLS IDENTIFICATION, TESTING, AND SELF-ASSESSMENT

___	Career Sort Assessment Instruments	$23.95 ___
___	Charting Your Goals	$12.95 ___
___	Discover the Right Job for You!	$11.95 ___
___	Discover What You're Best At	$11.95 ___
___	Quick Job Hunting Map	$3.95 ___
___	The Real-Life Aptitude Test	$10.95 ___
___	The Three Boxes of Life	$14.95 ___
___	The Truth About You	$11.95 ___
___	What Color Is Your Parachute?	$17.95 ___
___	Where Do I Go From Here With My Life?	$11.95 ___

RESEARCH ON JOBS, ORGANIZATIONS, CITIES, AND FIELDS

___	101 Careers	$12.95 ___
___	American Almanac of Jobs and Salaries	$15.95 ___
___	America's Phone Book	$24.95 ___
___	California	$9.95 ___
___	Career Finder	$9.95 ___
___	Careers Encyclopedia	$29.95 ___
___	Dictionary of Occupational Titles	$32.95 ___
___	Dictionary of Occupational Titles, 1986 Supplement	$7.95 ___
___	Directory of Executive Recruiters (1991)	$39.95 ___
___	Encyclopedia of Careers & Vocational Guidance	129.95 ___
___	Exploring Careers	$19.95 ___
___	Great Careers	$36.95 ___
___	Guide to Occupational Exploration	$36.95 ___
___	*"How to Be Happily Employed in..."* Boston, Dallas/Ft. Worth, San Francisco, Washington, DC ($10.95 each or $42.95 for set of 4)	$42.95 ___
___	*"How to Get a Job in..."* Atlanta, Chicago, Dallas/Ft. Worth, Houston, Los Angeles/San Diego, New York, San Francisco, Seattle/Portland, Washington, DC ($15.95 or $139.95 for set of 9)	$139.95 ___
___	*Job Bank Series:* Atlanta, Boston, Chicago, Dallas, Denver, Detroit, Florida, Houston, Los Angeles, Minneapolis, New York, Ohio, Philadelphia, San Francisco, Seattle, St. Louis, Washington, DC ($12.95 each or $219.95 for set of 17)	$219.95 ___
___	Jobs! What They Are, Where They Are...	$11.95 ___
___	Jobs 1991	$14.95 ___
___	Jobs Rated Almanac	$14.95 ___
___	National Trade and Professional Associations	$59.95 ___

___ Occupational Outlook Handbook $24.95   _____
___ Top Professionals $10.95   _____

RESUMES, LETTERS, AND NETWORKING

___ 200 Letters for Job Hunters $14.95   _____
___ Damn Good Resume Guide $7.95   _____
___ Does Your Resume Wear Apron Strings? $7.95   _____
___ Does Your Resume Wear Blue Jeans? $7.95   _____
___ Dynamite Cover Letters $9.95   _____
___ Dynamite Resumes $9.95   _____
___ Great Connections $11.95   _____
___ High Impact Resumes and Letters $12.95   _____
___ Is Your *"Net"* Working? $22.95   _____
___ Network Your Way to Job and Career Success $11.95   _____
___ Perfect Cover Letter $11.95   _____
___ Perfect Resume $11.95   _____
___ Resume Catalog $13.95   _____
___ Resumes That Knock 'Em Dead $7.95   _____
___ Sure-Hire Resumes $14.95   _____
___ Your First Resume $10.95   _____

DRESS, APPEARANCE, AND IMAGE

___ Color Me Beautiful $17.95   _____
___ Dress for Success $9.95   _____
___ Dressing Smart $19.95   _____
___ Professional Image $10.95   _____
___ Winner's Style $11.95   _____
___ Women's Dress for Success $8.95   _____
___ Working Wardrobe $11.95   _____

INTERVIEWS AND SALARY NEGOTIATIONS

___ Five Minute Interview $12.95   _____
___ How to Get Interviews From Job Ads $16.95   _____
___ How to Make $1,000 a Minute $7.95   _____
___ Interview for Success $11.95   _____
___ Salary Success $11.95   _____
___ Sweaty Palms $8.95   _____

PUBLIC-ORIENTED CAREERS

___ American Almanac of Government Jobs and Careers $14.95   _____
___ Compleat Guide to Finding Jobs in Government $14.95   _____
___ Complete Guide to Public Employment $15.95   _____
___ Find a Federal Job Fast! $9.95   _____
___ How to Get a Federal Job $15.00   _____
___ Profitable Careers in Nonprofit $12.95   _____

INTERNATIONAL AND OVERSEAS JOBS

___ Almanac of International Jobs and Careers $14.95   _____

___ Complete Guide to International Jobs and Careers	$13.95	_____
___ Guide to Careers in World Affairs	$11.95	_____
___ How to Get a Job in Europe	$15.95	_____
___ International Careers	$11.95	_____
___ International Jobs	$12.95	_____
___ Overseas List	$13.95	_____
___ Passport to Overseas Employment	$14.95	_____
___ Work, Study, Travel Abroad	$11.95	_____

MILITARY

___ Re-Entry	$13.95	_____
___ Retiring From the Military	$22.95	_____
___ Woman's Guide to Military Service	$10.95	_____
___ Young Person's Guide to the Military	$9.95	_____

WOMEN AND SPOUSES

___ Best Companies for Women	$9.95	_____
___ Careers for Women Without College	$10.95	_____
___ Getting Up When You're Feeling Down	$17.95	_____
___ Relocating Spouse's Guide to Employment	$12.95	_____

COLLEGE STUDENTS

___ College Majors and Careers	$16.95	_____
___ Graduating to the 9-5 World	$11.95	_____
___ Internships	$27.95	_____
___ Liberal Arts Jobs	$11.95	_____
___ Put Your Degree to Work	$9.95	_____

JOB LISTINGS AND NEWSLETTERS

___ Career Planning & Adult Development Newsletters (6 issues)	$30.00	_____
___ Career Opportunities News (6 issues)	$30.00	_____
___ Federal Career Opportunities (6 issues)	$37.00	_____
___ Federal Jobs Digest (6 issues)	$29.00	_____
___ International Employment Hotline (12 issues)	$29.00	_____

CHILDREN, YOUTH, AND SUMMER JOBS

___ It's Your Future	$11.95	_____
___ A Real Job for You	$9.95	_____
___ Teenager's Guide to the Best Summer Opportunities	$9.95	_____

MINORITIES, IMMIGRANTS, DISABLED

___ Black Woman's Career Guide	$14.95	_____
___ Directory of Special Programs for Minority Group Members	$34.95	_____
___ Finding A Job in the U.S.	$7.95	_____
___ Job Hunting For the Disabled	$10.95	_____
___ Yes You Can	$12.95	_____

EXPERIENCED AND ELDERLY

___ 40+ Job Hunting Guide	$21.95	___
___ Getting a Job After 50	$29.95	___

ALTERNATIVE CAREER FIELDS

___ *"Career Choices for the 90s"* Series (Art, Business, Communications/Journalism, Computer Science, Economics, English, History, Law, Mathematics, MBA, Political Science/Government, Psychology ($8.95 each or $99.95 for set of 12)	$99.95	
___ Career Opportunities in the Music Industry	$27.95	___
___ Careers in Accounting	$16.95	___
___ Careers in Business	$16.95	___
___ Careers in Communications	$16.95	___
___ Careers in Computers	$16.95	___
___ Careers in Education	$16.95	___
___ Careers in Engineering	$16.95	___
___ Careers in Health Care	$16.95	___
___ Careers in Science	$16.95	___
___ Careers With Robots	$26.95	___
___ Educator's Guide to Alternative Jobs & Careers	$13.95	___
___ Entrepreneur's Guide to Starting a Successful Business	$16.95	___
___ Flying High in Travel	$14.95	___
___ Job Opportunities for Business & Liberal Arts Graduates	$19.95	___
___ Job Opportunities for Engineering, Science, and Computer Graduates	$19.95	___
___ Making It in the Media Professions	$18.95	___
___ New Accountant Careers	$13.95	___
___ *"Opportunities in..."* Series (136+ titles: $12.95 each or $1749.95 set; contact publisher)	$1749.95	___
___ Outdoor Career Guide	$20.95	___
___ Planning Your Medical Career	$17.95	___

SUBTOTAL		___
Virginia residents add 4.5% sales tax		___
POSTAGE/HANDLING ($3.00 for first title and $.50 for each additional book)		$3.00 ___
TOTAL ENCLOSED		___